Leading Wisely

Leading Wisely

Becoming a Reflective Leader in Turbulent Times

Manfred F. R. Kets de Vries

WILEY

This edition first published 2022.

Registered office

John Wiley & Sons Ltd, The Atrium, Southern Gate, Chichester, West Sussex, PO19 8SQ, United Kingdom

For details of our global editorial offices, for customer services and for information about how to apply for permission to reuse the copyright material in this book please see our website at www.wiley.com.

Library of Congress Cataloging-in-Publication Data

Names: Kets de Vries, Manfred F. R., author.
Title: Leading wisely : becoming a reflective leader in turbulent times / Manfred F. R. Kets de Vries.
Description: Chichester, West Sussex, United Kingdom : Wiley, 2022. | Includes index.
Identifiers: LCCN 2021052110 (print) | LCCN 2021052111 (ebook) | ISBN 9781119860396 (hardback) | ISBN 9781119860419 (adobe pdf) | ISBN 9781119860402 (epub)
Subjects: LCSH: Leadership. | Wisdom.
Classification: LCC HD57.7 .K4794 2022 (print) | LCC HD57.7 (ebook) | DDC 658.4/092—dc23/eng/20211029
LC record available at https://lccn.loc.gov/2021052110
LC ebook record available at https://lccn.loc.gov/2021052111

Cover Design: Wiley
Cover Image: © Neoplantski/Shutterstock
Printed and bound by CPI Group (UK) Ltd, Croydon, CR0 4YY

C9781119860396_141221

Contents

Preface

> By three methods we can learn wisdom. First, by reflection which is noblest; second, by imitation, which is easiest; and third by experience, which is the bitterest.
>
> —Confucius.

> All truly wise thoughts have been thought already thousands of times; but to make them truly ours, we must think them over again honestly, until they take root in our personal experience.
>
> —Johann Wolfgang von Goethe

Being foolish

Aristotle is often attributed with the statement, 'There is a foolish corner in the brain of the wisest man.' One cannot help but wonder if he was thinking of something comparable to the idea of the so-called Darwin Awards competition. If you do not know what I am referring to, let me explain. The 'Darwin Award' is a rather tongue-in-cheek honor given to people who have singled themselves out by stupidly risking life and limb in the dumbest way possible. To be selected for this award, the following criteria must apply:

> In the spirit of Charles Darwin, the Darwin Awards commemorate individuals who protect our gene pool by making the ultimate sacrifice of their own lives by eliminating themselves in an extraordinarily idiotic manner, thereby improving our species' chances of long-term survival.

In other words, the candidate's foolishness must be unique and sensational. In fact, if the Darwin Awards does prove anything at all, it is that even presumably intelligent people can remove themselves from the gene pool in apparently ridiculous ways.

I remember how I could well have received an honorable citation for the Darwin Awards while canoeing with my wife and two children on the Concord River in Massachusetts. Due to the fast-melting snow, the river had completely flooded its banks. Large parts of what used to be land were now inundated. While happily paddling between the many trees that were now standing in the water, we came across a large, low hanging branch that was blocking our passage. Showing no judgement at all, I told everyone in the canoe to lean to one side to be able to pass under that branch, with the obvious result that the canoe keeled over and everyone suddenly spilled into the water. It was an amazingly stupid suggestion on my part.

Soaking wet, I fished the children out of the water and, for reasons of safety, put them on this infamous branch. Together with my wife – as we were able to stand in the overflowed river – we tilted the canoe to pour out the water. Subsequently, the two of us, completely soaked, paddled back to the shore like mad. When we got into our car, we put on maximum heat and drove home to Cambridge as fast as possible. We were lucky that we did not drown or catch pneumonia, but in future canoeing expeditions, I kept

William Blake's admonition in mind: 'A fool sees not the same tree that a wise man sees.' I had learned something the hard way. I had learned from experience. Never was such an accident going to happen to me again. In the future, I would have better judgement. In future actions, I would try to be wiser.

Beyond book learning

Even though I wrote this book only recently, in more than one way, these musings on wisdom in the context of leadership have been in the works for a very long time. In fact, it is fair to say that this book reflects the ruminations of my own struggles with foolishness, all the while trying to acquire a touch of wisdom. Although book learning has always been important to me, knowledge alone never seemed to be enough in dealing with many of the questions that I faced in my daily work as a professor, psychoanalyst, consultant and executive coach. Although I always thought that to acquire knowledge, studying does not hurt, to acquire wisdom, clearly something more was needed. Making efforts to appear knowledgeable did not seem to be good enough. Among other things, I realized that I needed to learn how to observe. If I wanted to act wisely, I needed to really make sense of what was going on around me. Fortunately, in that respect, my long psychoanalytic training turned out to be very useful.

Apart from needing to become more proficient in seeing things, much of what I have learned in life has also come to pass through the questioning of my students. These demanding interchanges – because, far too often, it had to do with questions to which there were no easy answers – were a good lesson in humility. Again and again, these discussions reminded me of my ignorance – it showed how little I really did know. In hindsight, I realized that I became even more aware of my limitations in sense making when I designed a program for C-suite executives at INSEAD, where I have been teaching for a very long time. Working with cohorts of C-suite executives from all over the globe proved to be even more of a challenge, compared to working with the much younger MBA students. Very often, the latter tended to be more gullible, while in many instances, the older executives would present me with extremely complex problems for which I had no easy answers.

For pedagogical reasons, most business schools use case studies. My approach has not been very different from that of the Harvard Business School – the epicenter of case studies – which is one of my alma maters. During a lifetime influenced by their pedagogical approach, I must have written over a hundred of these case studies. Frankly speaking, case studies have always been an excellent way to create the illusion of decision-making omnipotence – to provide students with the fantasy that they could tackle any difficult problem. Certainly, I was no exception, having once had similar illusions. After all, I had also at one time done an MBA. However, in this particular seminar, specifically designed for leaders of organizations, my approach became somewhat different. In this instance, I decided to take advantage of the fact that the interesting case studies were sitting right in my class. I came to realize that using my participants as prospective study subjects allowed me and others in the class to engage in a more in-depth way of sense making, compared to the traditional case study approach.

I should add that most case studies about senior executives are of a somewhat hagiographic nature, something I am very aware of, given my own case writing history. Why this is so, is that the protagonists in these case studies generally have 'the final cut', enabling them to take out of the case any information they do not fancy. Unfortunately, by doing so, the 'nerve is often taken out of the material'. In addition, to add to this 'cleansing process', I should mention the case writer's tendency towards self-censorship, his or her not wanting to include material that may seem to be too controversial, exactly because of the existence of this right of final cut. Furthermore, if truth be told, based on my own experience, it is rather rare for executives to truly open up in these case studies – to talk frankly about what is really troubling them. Getting them to go deep enough to tell a more complete story about the challenges they are facing in their lives is always an uphill struggle. After all, it is so much safer to keep the conversation at a rather superficial level.

In the seminars I designed, however, hagiography was not something that had a long life span. As the objective of the program is to help participants develop deeper insights about themselves – to find ways to navigate through life's challenging situations – staying merely on the surface is not really an option. It would be difficult to keep the discussions going by remaining at a superficial level. As a matter of fact, it would be a real waste of time. Yet, most participants tended to open up, as their defenses wore down. Gradually, they would pay more heed to the statement 'no interpretation without association'. They would come to realize that if they kept the discussion merely at a superficial level, they would not get much out of such a seminar. To go beyond superficialities was in their best interest. Of course, what facilitated the process of having the participants really open up was that their colleague-participants were becoming increasingly effective in identifying what was happening beneath the surface. As time went by, what would come to the surface were the real issues that the person 'in the hot seat' was trying to deal with.

During these sessions, many insightful questions, reflections and insights would come to the fore. Although there is nothing bad about learning from one's own experience, learning from the experience of others can be of equal merit. Looking back, having facilitated these kinds of seminars for a very long time, I can only say that it has been a great learning adventure. Much wisdom was always present during these sessions.

More than a decade ago, encouraged by what I learned from my students during these seminars, I wrote a book with the title, *Sex, Money, Happiness, and Death: Musings from the Underground*, where I reflected on the insights provided to me by my participants. Quite recently, as the COVID-19 pandemic has offered me much more time for reflection, this particular book has been followed by five others: *Journeys into Coronavirus Land: Lessons from a Pandemic*; *The CEO Whisperer: Meditations on Leadership, Life and Change*; *Quo Vadis?*: *The Existential Challenges of Leaders*; *Leadership Unhinged: Essays on the Ugly, the Bad and the Weird* and *Dancing on Quicksand: The Daily Perils of Executive Life*. Looking back, one important issue that runs like a red thread through these three books is how to make wise decisions.

A 'clinical' orientation

The importance of wisdom as a guiding principle led me to reflect on the kind of conceptual schemes that I have been using in trying to make sense of the stories my participants would tell me. This pertains to the question of what kind of lenses I apply to understand the deeper meaning of what my participants are dealing with. Added to this is another question of particular importance: while using these lenses, how can I weave together into a cohesive pattern the emerging thoughts, feelings and behavior patterns that come my way?

To start with, as a management professor, there is my knowledge of organizational life. However, to only use this organizational lens to help understand what the executives in my seminars are trying to present would provide a rather one-sided, two-dimensional picture of their lives. Therefore, I have found another lens to be extremely useful. It came from putting on my hat as a psychoanalyst. Through the use of a more psychodynamic-systemic oriented lens – thus having a more clinical orientation to the making sense of things – I began to pay attention to not only what is happening in people's lives on the surface but also what is happening beneath the surface. After all, as a clinician, I have always been interested not only in conscious phenomena, but also in what happens at an unconscious level. Putting on this more 'clinical' hat has always been an important part of my way of making sense of the world. It helped me to deal better with the 'wisdom equation', to become more reflective in my decision making.

Wisdom and society

By and large, people who realize the importance of wisdom will make better decisions during their life's journey. They appreciate how wisdom can be an enabler. They realize the importance of wise decisions for their individual and social well-being. They realize that, without wise decisions, their societies will be at risk, but they are also quite aware of how much wisdom is still lacking in our present-day world, despite our great advances in knowledge.

It is for all to see that, on a fundamental level, the tragedy of the human condition has not lessened. We still are not able to get things right. *Homo sapiens* continues to make a mess of things. Presently, our sense of alienation – manifested through feelings of powerlessness, normlessness, and meaninglessness – appears to be at an all-time high. Fear, anxiety, and depression are ever-present, and related to this flood of emotional distress, epidemics of addictive behavior can be seen everywhere. Added to this sorry state of affairs, we are still living in a world full of conflict with large groups of people still exposed to much starvation and war. Sadly enough, the only difference between the past and the present seems to be the difference between throwing stones and shooting high powered, nuclear missiles. Notwithstanding these tragic developments, many of us live with the illusion that if we were to amass just a little bit more knowledge, everything would be all right. Unfortunately, very little thought is given to the greater accumulation of wisdom – how to make wiser decisions.

Sadly enough, while we are living in an information society where knowledge is omnipresent, we are still living in a world where wisdom is direly lacking. Clearly, in our current world, we are able to gather information and knowledge at a much faster rate than we are able to gather wisdom. Referring again to the idea of a 'wisdom equation' in leadership, there is no question but that wise leaders are rare and far between. Many of our present leaders are everything but paragons of wisdom. Frankly speaking, far too many of them are not up to the challenge. They are behaving more like actors in a reality show, trying to peddle their illusions. They are catering to what people 'wish to believe', but are unable to give wise council to their citizens. Populists as they are, many of them promise unrealistic, overly simplistic miracle cures to deal with the ills of society. They seem to be in the 'fan fiction' business, creating fantasy facts and alternative realities. It seems that the ignorant and the belligerent have the upper hand, and it is easy to recognize that in their actions, wisdom is direly lacking. Even worse, it often seems that the less wisdom they show, the more popular they are. The fewer facts they present, the more they push 'dream politics', the more they are applauded. The more factoids they present, invented out of thin air, the more they dazzle their followers.

These demagogue-like leaders are not concerned about what is in the best interest from a communal/societal point of view. They are not interested in the common good. Far too many of them only seem to be in pursuit of their self-interest. In other words, they are just looking out for number one. If we take a hard look at their behavior, it would become clear that most of them lack a moral compass. They are anything but value driven. However, where they do excel is in their capacity to take advantage of the dearth of wisdom among their followers. They seem to be acutely aware of the fact that wisdom does not emerge out of collective ignorance, but aiming for the lowest *Zeitgeist* denominator is not the answer to solving the complex problems that humankind is facing.

Many of these leaders seem to have forgotten that the greatness of a nation is not measured in dollars and cents but in human decency. What makes a country great should not be a simple transactional calculation. To be possessed by the forces of selfishness and greed – individual or national – is not the answer in dealing with the serious ills of society. On the contrary, well-functioning societies have a set of values that define them.

It is quite disturbing that in these very turbulent times, when enlightened leadership is needed more than ever, a country's citizens – confused and excited as they may be – are more likely to respond to the siren calls of these demagogue-like leaders while refusing to listen to the voice of wisdom. The results are there for all to see. Unfortunately, as has been said all too often, hundreds of wise men cannot make the world a heaven, but one idiot is enough to turn it into a hell. The philosopher Bertrand Russell put it quite astutely: 'The whole problem with the world is that fools and fanatics are always so certain of themselves, and wiser people so full of doubts.'

All in all, the main reason I am writing this book about wisdom is that in this confusing world of ours, characterized by volatility, uncertainty, complexity and ambiguity, I am trying to make a plea for more wisdom in leadership. As I have suggested, looking at the state of the world, many of our present leaders are not the role models we would like to emulate. On the contrary, we need different kinds of leaders. I am referring to the kinds of people who prefer love above hatred, who are able to foster harmony, instead of divisiveness, who are advocates of peace, not of war, and who prefer to build bridges, not walls. Furthermore, we should be on the lookout for leaders of integrity, who advocate justice, not corruption and lawlessness. While I may sound naïve, I am also referring to the kinds of leaders for whom concepts like freedom, care, values and character do matter. We should never forget that freedom flourishes upon the bedrock of ethics and integrity, not hypocrisy. In particular, we need leaders who build social trust, not distrust. In high trust societies, good things happen. Leaders who cherish these values will be the life blood of any true democracy.

In our present-day world characterized by a pandemic, global warming, nuclear threats, terrorism and dramatic income inequalities, we need more than ever leaders who are interested in promoting knowledge and wisdom, not ignorance. We need leaders who transcend people's wish to believe. I am referring to the kind of people who are reality driven, who have a solid grasp of what is possible and are interested in doing things for the common good. It is exactly this kind of leadership that will prevent us from entering doomsday scenarios.

Notwithstanding the many threats that we are facing in this day-and-age, far too many people still do not realize the importance of wisdom for the advancement of humanity. They do not realize that time is running out if we want to save our planet. It is here exactly where wise leaders can make a difference. When leaders possess a degree of wisdom, their actions can contribute to real transformation, a process that is not merely a redecoration of the past but a transformation of humanity that embodies the eternally new.

My agenda

As I have mentioned before, this book should be seen within the context of my discussions with my students about what lessons of life have been important to them in running their organizations. I kept on asking them, as a leader, what would they do to be more effective? What could they do to contribute to creating a better world? What words of wisdom had stuck with them?

In distilling the essence of these discussions, for reasons of simplicity, I have decided to limit myself to eight lessons that pertain to wisdom in the context of leadership and other life challenges. I am quite cognizant of the fact that I could have included more lessons on wisdom, but many of the additional lessons are intertwined within the others. Wisdom, in the end, is a kind of enigma and we need to recognize that from the start. To that end, I have added three chapters upfront where I present some of my more general reflections pertaining to the wisdom equation.

Furthermore, to clarify even more what I want to say, I have included many short stories and anecdotes originating from China, Japan, the Middle East and Europe. The main protagonists in these stories are the Buddha, Zen masters, Aesop (a storyteller believed to have lived in ancient Greece) and mullah Nasrudin (a wise man born in present-day Turkey). Also, included are anecdotes from the Old Testament, the brothers Grimm and a few more contemporary tales. In addition, in each chapter I have added a number of questions to help the reader further explore the various themes that are being discussed.

Given the clinical lens that I often use to make sense of the puzzles that life presents to us, it is important to note that wisdom lies not just in seeing things but also in seeing through things. Of course, it often requires wisdom to recognize wisdom. When touching on this subject, I like to tell my students that the gateways of wisdom are always open, but you have to be willing to walk through them. Moreover, while taking this walk, you need to be prepared to make wise choices. You need to be able to set your priorities wisely. In that respect, the following story could be quite illuminating:

> A professor stood before his philosophy class to begin his lecture. To start his class – without saying a word – he picked up a very large and empty bowl and proceeded to fill it up with large pebbles. Having done so, he asked the students if the bowl was full. All of them agreed that it was the case. Giving his students a big smile, their professor then picked up a bag of sand, to put them in the bowl. Quite easily, the sand found space between the pebbles. Again, the professor asked the students if the bowl was full. Once more, all of them thought that the bowl would now be completely full.
>
> Subsequently, the professor took out a jar of water, to also pour it into the bowl. Without difficulties, the water found space between the pebbles and the sand. Sounding like a broken record, the professor asked once again if the bowl was full. Somewhat surprised, the students responded affirmatively.
>
> 'Now,' said the professor, as they stopped smiling. 'Look at the way I handled the pebbles, sand and water as your journey through life. These big pebbles are the important things you're dealing with. I am thinking of your family, your friends, your health, your passions and your concerns for society at large. The things that make for a full and complete life. The sand represents the other

things that matter, like your job, your house, your car and various other things.'

'The water is everything else – the smaller stuff. If you put the water into the bowl first,' he continued, 'there is no room for the sand or the pebbles. The same can be said about your life. If you spend all your time and energy on the smaller stuff, you will never have room for the things that are really important to you. It doesn't show wisdom. Thus, always pay attention to the things that make a difference; the things that make you feel alive. Consequently, have a good relationship with your partner. Enjoy the time of playing with your children. Try to maintain good relationships with your friends. Don't forget to take care of your health. Furthermore, pursue your desire to create a better society. There will always be time to take care of the smaller things. Make the pebbles your first priority – those are the things that really matter. Keep on reminding yourself that the sand and the water are of much less importance.'

1

Not knowing

Knowledge is learning something new every day. Wisdom is letting go of something every day.

—Zen proverb

The fool doth think he is wise, but the wise man knows himself to be a fool.

—William Shakespeare

Not knowing

According to Plato, the renowned Greek philosopher Socrates went to this temple of Apollo in ancient Thebes and asked the Pythia, the Oracle, 'Who is the wisest person in Athens.' The oracle replied, 'It is you.'

'That is impossible,' said Socrates, 'because I am aware that I know nothing.'

'That,' said the Oracle, 'is exactly why you are the wisest person in Athens.'

Socrates recognized that there was so much he did not know. Knowing this, however, may have been precisely the reason that made him wiser than all the others. It was this awareness of his own ignorance that differentiated him. Thus, in a rather paradoxical way, Socrates expressed that he knew nothing except that he knew that he knew nothing – in short, he recognized the many unknowns in his world. However, does the possession of wisdom imply knowing that you don't know? Is it the acceptance of your own ignorance? Thus, the greatest wisdom may very well lie in the explicit recognition that one is not all knowing.

Hopefully, you have entered a stage of life when you realize how little you know. Of course, you may think, somewhat nostalgically, about your younger years when you thought that you knew everything, but if you are truly in pursuit of wisdom, these thoughts will be fleeting. Only when you realize how little you really know will you make the effort to continue trying to understand what the world has to offer. Eventually, like Socrates, you may have figured out that knowledge is infinite, that knowledge changes at all times, and that all knowledge is transient as it is linked to the world around it. Therefore, knowledge is subject to change as the world is ever in the process of changing. It is for exactly this reason that Socrates felt compelled to continue searching for new knowledge and to understand things even better. This never-ending pursuit of knowledge may have been undertaken with the hope that wisdom eventually would be within reach. To attain it, however, was going to be another story. Wisdom has this infuriating tendency to always remain untouchable.

A wise old man, a guest of the king, spent his days dressed magnificently, eating the greatest delicacies at the king's table. The advisers sought his advice and the powerful laughed heartily at his jokes, while the relatives of the king showered him with gifts.

A party of young, arrogant noblemen met the old man one day amidst the lush trees within the royal garden and challenged him about his wisdom: 'Now tell us Seeker of the Truth, given all the things you know, how many grains of sand would fit in this bucket?'

'My apologies, your fine noblemen, I haven't the faintest idea.'

'Well, how disappointing! But let's ask you something else. Can you tell us this simple thing: Why can you see in a mirror your right and left eye and ear reversed in the reflection but not your face upside down?'

'If I only knew, you priceless offspring of your eminent fathers.'

But the young noblemen didn't know how to stop pestering the wise old man. 'Then, tell us at the least, what is the meaning of life?'

'As far as that's concerned, I only know that I don't know, your very honorable people.'

At this point, the young noblemen exclaimed: 'You don't know this, and you don't know that! Why then are you, silly, old man, fed and dressed and honored at the royal tables as if you were the wisest of all people?'

'Oh, your noble people,' replied the old man, 'I am dressed in silk and fed with good food only for the little that I know. For if I were to be rewarded for what I don't know, all the treasuries of the world put together would not be sufficient.'

Defining wisdom

Socrates did not really define what wisdom meant to him and what would be its various components. Frankly speaking, defining what wisdom is all about is difficult. Wisdom is of a rather ethereal nature. It cannot really be taught; it cannot just be mere knowledge. It is not just intelligence. Although we recognize that when referring to wisdom, knowledge and intelligence may play a role and we also realize that wisdom is a much more complex entity.

Generally speaking, we feel compelled to acquire knowledge as a way of trying to control the chaos that is life. To gain knowledge can be seen as part of our efforts to make sense of things. In many instances, it is knowledge that we search for when looking for deliverance from our human predicament. We have the hope that knowledge will give us clear answers to existential questions. Frequently, however, knowledge can also be used to mask our biases and to disguise our value judgments. Sadly enough, much of the knowledge we acquire may be misleading, irrelevant, and inaccurate. In the end, it may prove incapable of helping us make sense of whatever difficult challenges we have to deal with. Moreover, the world we live in is now full of factoids or alternative facts that are often presented as knowledge – in other words, 'knowledge' that turns out to blatantly false. We may also have discovered that making wise decisions in the 'real world' necessitates often something more than just possessing raw knowledge. As the Roman poet Horace would point out, 'wisdom is not wisdom when it is derived from books alone.' To be wise implies having the ability to interpret and act on complex situations, aided by whatever knowledge we have acquired. Unfortunately, resorting merely to knowledge does not necessarily make for wise decisions and actions.

Switching from the concept of knowledge to that of intelligence, we are faced with a similar conundrum. All too often, highly intelligent people can be seen acting in remarkably unintelligent ways. What this tells us is that mere intelligence – like knowledge – may not be enough to decipher the puzzle that is wisdom. As the Russian writer Fyodor Dostoyevsky once said, 'Intelligence alone is not nearly enough when it comes to acting wisely.'

Perhaps a better way of looking at the wisdom conundrum is to define it more as the appropriate, more discerned application of whatever knowledge we possess – the ability to judge complex problems correctly and to subsequently follow the best course of action based on the knowledge that we have available. In other words, having wisdom also includes the anticipation of consequences of our actions – it being a reflection of how well we are dealing with a specific situation.

Actually, taking a somewhat more 'rational', scientific approach, we could define wisdom as being an advanced cognitive and emotional developmental state that is experience driven and, when applied, always takes the common good into consideration. Although this definition may sound forbidding, what I am suggesting is that wisdom seems to be composed of three structural components: a talent in cognitive and emotional integration that helps to solve complex issues, the ability to take the appropriate actions, and the concern that whatever actions are taken will have a positive effect on others and also ourselves.

Hopefully, a better understanding of what wisdom is all about is beginning to materialize. I imagine, however, that there is still somewhat of a confusion given our tendency – at least in general discourse – to use the terms being knowledgeable, being intelligent, and having wisdom, somewhat interchangeably. Thus, it does not always make it easy to distinguish one from the other. Far too often, knowledge, intelligence, and wisdom seem to be intertwined.

In an attempt to further unravel this conundrum, I should add that you are not born with knowledge. On the contrary, you acquire knowledge. In other words, being knowledgeable is an experiential phenomenon, meaning that knowledge is what you know. You should view it as the sum of everything that you have learned over the years. Clearly, knowledge will grow and change along with you.

In contrast, intelligence can be described as a measure of how much you understand. It refers to your intellectual or mental capacity. In other words, if you are intelligent, it will be relatively easy to learn new skills, solve problems effectively, as well as comprehend complex ideas. Thus, a large part of intelligence (being really smart) is the result of genetics. I should add, however, that intelligence also has a developmental component. The kind of learning experiences provided to you while growing up also plays a role. How well you use your intelligence very much depends on the interplay of nature and nurture. To recapitulate, in making a comparison between intelligence and knowledge, it is important to note that you can be very intelligent and still not know very much, while you can be very knowledgeable and still be mostly unintelligent.

Wisdom, by contrast, is a very different entity. Though related to knowledge and intelligence, it is more abstract and subjective. While knowledge and intelligence can be measured to some extent, wisdom is not really quantifiable. It has more of a qualitative nature. It pertains to a subjective measure of the quality of your insights.

What I am also suggesting is that mere knowledge onto itself can be a very sterile proposition. Furthermore, having acquired much knowledge because you happen to be intelligent does not necessarily make you wise. In comparison, it is wisdom that will bring you into a very different orbit. As the philosopher Alfred North Whitehead puts it quite nicely: 'Knowledge shrinks as wisdom grows.' Wisdom pertains to other ways of knowing or other ways of being intelligent. Unlike knowledge, which is acquired, wisdom comes from within. With the danger of sounding overly simplistic: wisdom has to do with using your common sense to an uncommon degree. It has to do with your talent in judging appropriately the truth and the validity of your accumulated knowledge.

Wisdom implies that you have the power of discernment, that you can judge properly as to what are the right or wrong things to do. It pertains to your ability to pair your accumulated knowledge and synthesize this knowledge using your moral understanding of the situation. Furthermore, wisdom is knowing what to do with your knowledge – how to use your understanding wisely – as well as recognizing the limits of your knowledge. Thus, another way to define wisdom is the ability to see into the future the consequences of your choices in the present – to know when to take action and when it is useless even to try. It makes knowledge the child of (frequently difficult) experiences.

Once upon a time there was a king who offered an award to the artist who could create the painting that would best symbolize the idea of wisdom. Not surprisingly, the competition created great excitement in the kingdom. Many artists were eager to submit their works. When the day arrived to exhibit all the works, the king looked carefully at each of the paintings. After much thought, he selected two paintings as the finalists. Having seen the paintings, his subjects wondered which one of the two he was going to choose.

One painting portrayed a peaceful lake surrounded by beautiful green meadows and framed above by a perfectly blue sky. At first sight, everyone really liked this painting. It gave all the viewers a very tranquil, reflective feeling. The serenity of the study put people's mind to rest. Most people felt that the scenery portrayed in the painting was a very nice way to symbolize wisdom.

The other painting was totally different. It portrayed a windswept, rainy landscape, overcast with stormy clouds, the scenery further divided by a raging river that, due to the storm, was overflowing its banks. There was nothing restful about this imagery. But to everyone's surprise, after giving it much thought, the king selected this painting.

Everyone was wondering why? When asked, the king told his subjects to look very closely. When they didn't see what he wanted them to see, he pointed out that in the corner of the painting there was a small rainbow to be seen. Under the rainbow was a little cave – and if you looked very, very carefully, you saw that, beside the cave, a mother bear and her two cubs were peacefully at rest.

The king explained, saying that wisdom doesn't emerge from a place where there is no noise, no trouble or no challenges. Wisdom derives from knowing how to keep your cool in the midst of a storm.

Acquiring night vision

As I am suggesting, many very knowledgeable and highly intelligent people lack wisdom. Clearly, to acquire knowledge as opposed to wisdom requires very different methods of exploration. Of course, you can study many books to attain greater knowledge, but to study books to attain wisdom will be much more of a challenge. As the German-Swiss novelist Hermann Hesse explains, 'Knowledge can be communicated, but not wisdom. One can find it, live it, be fortified by it, do wonders through it, but one cannot communicate and teach it.' To acquire wisdom, you must be willing to observe, experience and act, using the best of your judgement. That is the reason any effort to obtain a modicum of wisdom necessitates a very different curriculum, as the story of the king and the painting illustrates. To read books, helpful as such an activity may be, would not be sufficient.

Wisdom also implies acquiring a degree of 'night vision', meaning having the ability to see what is not so obvious and not to be fooled by superficialities. Many people imagine that they see. In truth, however, they do not really observe. As a result, they do not understand. Generally speaking, people do not see beyond the surface of things; they are used to judging a book by its cover. However, while doing so, they do not see what is happening beneath the surface. What I am trying to say is that wisdom is not increased by acquiring more information, but rather by increasing the capacity of your seeing.

Sadly enough, many people do not understand the root causes of behaviors and actions. They remain blind to the fascinating world of unconscious phenomena. They do not know how to decipher the subliminal signs. However, there are ways to go about it. In the Preface of this book, I have already mentioned the psychodynamic-systemic lens that I use to add another dimension to the understanding of complex phenomena – in being able to observe things better. For the wisdom equation, such a lens may be a *sine qua non*.

Clearly, to acquire wisdom, you need to be able to see not only what is on the surface, but also what is beneath it. Unfortunately, as I have mentioned before, most people only see the obvious. Of course, they may have become quite knowledgeable about various subjects by reading, researching and memorizing facts. They may even be able to spout knowledge. Being able to do so makes them seem intelligent. It makes them look clever. However, what should be kept in mind is that people who have all the answers are not necessarily wise. In spite of being perceived as knowledgeable, they may be totally blind to many things. In contrast, wise people are less certain about what is going on in their lives. They may have their doubts in trying to make sense of what is happening around them. As the Persian poet Jalāl ad-Dīn Muhammad Rūmī said, 'Sell your cleverness and buy bewilderment.' They very much realize that there is so much that they do not know. There are so many mysteries that need to be deciphered, but it is exactly this particular state of mind that makes them curious to want to learn more. Therefore, it should not come as a surprise that in their wanderings through life, they keep on registering a sense of wonder and bewilderment.

Sometimes, I wonder whether our wisdom tends to grow in proportion to our awareness of our ignorance. After all, like Socrates, only when we realize that we know so very little will we continue to be searching for greater knowledge. It is exactly the acknowledgement of our ignorance – of all these unknowns – that might motivate us to search for more. In reflecting on this search for more, a Zen story about a Zen master and a prospective student comes to my mind:

A visitor went to see a Zen master to request him to impart spiritual knowledge to help him to become wise. The Zen master asked him to sit down to have a cup of tea. After he had placed the cup in front of the visitor, he started to pour. Quickly the cup filled up, but the Zen master didn't stop. He kept on pouring, causing the tea to spill out.

Seeing what was happening, the visitor became increasingly agitated, to finally cry out: 'Please stop, the cup is full. Don't you see that the tea is running out of the cup?'

The Zen master replied, 'Why don't you look at the cup as a metaphor of your mind. The way you spoke to me, it seems like your cup is already completely full. But how, when you think that you already know everything, can you become receptive to new knowledge? How could I ever help you to become wise?'

As this Zen story suggests, wisdom does not come to people who believe that they have nothing more to learn. After all, you cannot really explore the universe if you think that you are the center of it. If you desire to grow and develop, you should have a never-ending need for a greater understanding of what is happening around you. In particular, if you are looking for wisdom, it is important to always remain curious. You should never let go of this compelling need to find out more about all the unknowns.

Personal qualities

Having wisdom also suggests the possession of an array of personal qualities that will vary in relevance. Among the ones often cited as part of the wisdom equation are compassion, empathy, authenticity, open-mindedness, flexible thinking, humility, judgement, emotional intelligence, courage, curiosity, love of learning and kindness. Obviously, some of these qualities will be more important than others – as I will show in the subsequent discussion. Generally speaking, however, what these qualities suggest is that wise people are quite perceptive in making sense of the human dilemmas faced by themselves and other people. They quickly understand the issues that they are struggling with and are able to give well thought through action recommendations.

What should also be added is that wise people appear to be less interested in going after purely hedonistic pursuits. What is more top of mind, is the pursuit of the common good, meaning activities that also would benefit other people besides themselves. As they like their actions to transcend their self-interests, they are guided by a strong moral compass in whatever actions they undertake. Generally speaking, wise people possess a strong set of values. They possess a true-north moral compass. In other words, wise people try to do what they think is right, not what is going to be easy. As the Roman statesman Cicero said quite simply, 'The function of wisdom is to discriminate between good and evil.'

Furthermore, given their sense of curiosity about the world, people wanting to pursue wisdom are more likely to engage in cerebral activities. Self-reflection, self-knowledge and personal growth will be important to them, and while they are learning from experience, they try to acquire a rich understanding of how the world they live in really functions. In fact, the way they display their wisdom often invites admiration and encouragement.

While further reflecting on the story of the king and the stormy painting, keep in mind that storms can purify the atmosphere, enabling you to have a much clearer sight afterwards. What is more, quite frequently – as the king in the story recognized – often it is wisdom that turns out to be the child of these storms. In fact, without experiencing internal storms, it will be difficult for you to obtain the calmness of wisdom. Only by making sense of intense life experiences will wisdom come your way. However, it does not completely explain the ultimate motivation to search for wisdom. Why do we experience this need to know all these unknowns?

The 'stealth motivator' that is death

As far as unknowns are concerned, death can be viewed as the final unknown. Death can be considered the ultimate mystery. However, given its mystifying nature, the knowledge of the inevitability of death may be an explanatory factor in your desire to acquire wisdom. Thus, at a certain point in your life, you may come to realize that the greatest mystery of your life is that it ends. That being so, it could well become the driving force for greater exploration.[1] You may decide that whatever you are doing deserves greater scrutiny. As Socrates said very astutely, 'The unexamined life is not worth living.' When you are aware of endings, the fear of living an unlived life will become more pressing. If you have lived your life in such a manner, it will begin to feel like the last thing that you would like to happen. Therefore, could it be that the need to pursue wisdom is driven by the will to live life in such a way that you are prepared to face death when it comes? Could it be that your preoccupation with wisdom is based on the wish to unveil life's ultimate mystery?

---

[1] Manfred F. R. Kets de Vries (2014). Death and the executive: Encounters with the "stealth" motivator, *Organizational Dynamics*, 43 (4), 247–256.

The ever-presence of death may also lead you to question what you really want out of life. What would make your life truly meaningful? The reminder that you are mortal may even tempt you to ask the tough questions about your life such as, 'Who am I?' 'Why am I here?' 'What drives me?' 'Is this the kind of life I want to live?' 'What would I like to accomplish in the life that I have left?' If you are prepared to address these questions – if you do not want to live an unexamined life – you might find yourself walking on unexplored, but interesting paths. Also, in trying to deal with these questions, you may be forced to become more honest with yourself about the way that you are living. It may even motivate you to ask yourself, 'What would you consider a life, well-lived?' and 'What changes, sacrifices and actions are you prepared to make to be able to live a fully lived life?'

It could very well be that once you realize the finality of life, you liberate yourself from letting life merely pass by. No longer will you live under the illusion that you have an infinite amount of time; that you can put off until some future date the need to understand what is bringing significance to your life. Instead, the inevitability of your impending death may teach you many things about the wise use of your time – about the various challenges that warrant your attention.

Most likely, given the statement, 'Dust thou art, and to dust thou shalt return,' many of us would like to fill our lives with meaningful activities. In fact, it is quite paradoxical that as soon as we become truly aware of the fact that life has an ending, we begin to appreciate what life has to offer.[2] Once more, death anxiety encourages us to explore what our life is

[2] Manfred F. R. Kets de Vries (2021). *Quo Vadis? The Existential Challenges of Leaders*. London: Palgrave.

all about. Thus, knowing that there may come a day when our life will be flashing before our eyes, we want to make sure that whatever passes by is going to be worth watching.

Of course, some people may be obsessed by the idea of an after-life. It becomes their way to alleviate their anxiety about death. In the meantime, however, it is wise to explore what is happening in *this* life. Hopefully, in the pursuit of wisdom, they may find what is meaningful to them. Their challenge will be to realize what is really important – how to direct their energy – before they approach their end. Otherwise, they may end up living a life of regrets.

Looking for answers

If you possess this attitude of not knowing, you will also be better equipped to deal with situations whereby you do not know the answer to a question. Wise people accept it as something to look forward to, seeing it as yet another learning opportunity. Consequently, wise people astutely take advantage of difficult questions. They will truly welcome questions to which they have no answers. It forces them to reflect on what is being said. As I have learned from experience, it is exactly these questions that contribute to new insights. In fact, the people who are truly experts – the ones respected by other experts – are the first to admit how much there is yet to be discovered. Thus, what may need repeating, recalling Socrates' remarks, is that true wisdom is found in your admitting to not knowing. It also has to do with your ability to see – and to see what is beyond the obvious. In that respect, a true sign of wisdom is to constantly wonder about things, to take nothing for granted, and to be less sure that you understand the challenges that come your way.

Wise people always keep in mind that nobody has a monopoly on the truth. In fact, they are more like passengers in a train, travelling within the landscape of wisdom, trying to catch an occasional glimpse of what could be an insight. While travelling through this landscape, they know that there are many forces trying to pull them in different directions, but they also realize, while on this journey, that the best they can do is to be tolerant of these forces. Confusing as it might be, they also know that these forces reflect what the universe has to offer. However, even though these forces will create moments of paralysis, wise people also realize that they cannot let it be. The images glanced at during this train journey should be translated into action. Wise people know that there will be times when they have to take a stand, to do what they think is right.

While pursuing wisdom, you can look at your life as a book with many chapters. This book of life will also contain much data; it will have many facts. However, your challenge will be to discern the lessons that are embedded within all the facts that can be found in your book of life. In your search for wisdom, will you be able to untangle among these many facts the stories of success and failure, of joy and sorrow? Can you make sense out of them? Have you learned something from the stormy moments that you went through? Are you able to see any patterns? Does what you have learned, given these stormy experiences, help you in making wise decisions? Are you engaged in any activities that go beyond the self? Are you following Albert Einstein's admonition: 'Only a life lived for others is a life worthwhile.'

Furthermore, wise people, in aiming for the common good, will not be afraid to raise their voice for honesty and truth and compassion against the forces of injustice, selfishness and greed. If such behavior was to become contagious – if people all over the world were prepared to share their values – it could change the world. In other words, a country's greatest treasure could be the presence of citizens that possess wisdom. This begs the question of what leaders can do to imbue more wisdom into society. How can they prevent ignorance from gaining the upper hand? Unfortunately, as I mentioned in the Preface, looking at the present state of our world, the future of humankind seems to be dependent on the outcome of the race between the growing power of our technology vis-à-vis the wisdom of how to use it. How we can ensure that wisdom will 'win' will ultimately be our real challenge.

Thus, my question to you, the reader, is what have you done recently with respect to the wisdom equation? What activities are you involved in – even if it is only baby steps – towards the pursuit of wisdom? If you are in a leadership position, what are you doing presently to improve people's lives in the organization/community/society you are working in? Furthermore, in trying to make your contribution towards a more liveable world, what are *you* doing to make sure that wisdom is going to 'win'?

2

Beyond book knowledge

Fortune truly helps those who are of good judgement.

—Euripides

Wisdom is the daughter of experience.

—Leonardo da Vinci

Allow me to begin with a tale:

Once upon a time, there was a wise woman, who while picking mushrooms in the woods, found a large gold nugget lying under the moss. She picked up the nugget and brought it home. Soon after, a traveller knocked at her door asking her if he could stay for the night. The woman was very happy to do so. But when preparing food for the traveller, her visitor saw the gold nugget lying on the table. Realizing its value, he asked her if he could have it. Without any hesitation, the woman handed the nugget over to him. Extremely happy with the gift, the traveller left the next day, planning to go to the city to sell the gold nugget.

A few days later the traveller knocked once more on the door of the wise woman. When she opened the door, he said to her: 'When I was walking back to the city to sell the gold nugget, I couldn't stop thinking about your generosity. You must have known that the nugget is extremely valuable, that it's worth a lot of money. I hadn't told you, when I stayed at your place, that I need money badly. I now wonder whether you understood my predicament, given how kind you were to give me this gold nugget.'

'But while I was walking to the city, I came to realize that what's more valuable than this nugget is what you have within you. What do you have within you that made you so spontaneously give me that gold nugget? How did you understand how needy and greedy I was? What gave you the wisdom to let go of this nugget? It makes me wonder what makes you so satisfied with what you have. Thus, I came back to have you help me understand what special gift you possess. It is a gift that I really would like to have.'

As the traveller in this story seemed to become all too well aware, gold dust may be precious, but when it gets into your eyes, it will obstruct your vision. He may have been shrewd in getting hold of the gold nugget, but did he have wisdom? Later on, however, reflecting on the actions of the wise woman, he came to recognize that wisdom outweighs any wealth. He may have concluded that wisdom was much better than wealth, because wisdom can protect you, while you have to guard your wealth. Moreover, wealth decreases if you spend it, but the more you make use of wisdom, the more it tends to increase. Furthermore, what you get through wealth is gone once the wealth itself has gone, but what you achieve through wisdom often remains, even after you are gone. Often, it is what leaving a legacy is all about. The philosopher Friedrich Nietzsche said it quite well: 'He who has a why to live can bear almost any how.'

Wisdom's other colours

As wise people have made a great effort to know themselves, they are more prepared to accept and even embrace the differences between themselves and others. They take much more time to digest these contradictions to understand what these differences are really telling them. In addition, they try to learn from people who have different opinions even if they do not necessarily agree with them. It is exactly this talent in considered sense making that goes beyond paying attention to mere factual matters – beyond the simple acquisition of knowledge. It is exactly this kind of understanding that brings what would have been mere intelligence into another dimension.

You may have discovered for yourself that both knowledgeable and intelligent people can be very quick in expressing their opinion on various matters. Quite often, however, these people are just trying to be clever, but given their need to come across as clever, they are more likely to stick to their opinions, making for a greater degree of closed-mindedness. They may not be as open to new experiences and, to add insult to injury, they often like to impose their opinions on other people.

Compared to wise people, these clever people may pay greater attention to raw knowledge. In that respect, they are quite fact oriented, processing information in a quite logical and systematic fashion. Furthermore, although they may come across as much more confident about all the things that they are able to do, their presumed self-confidence is often a veneer for a great amount of insecurity. As a matter of fact, they may use arrogance as a defense. However, what seems to be missing is humility, an important part of the wisdom equation.

The significance of humility

Mulla Nasrudin is a traditional Middle Eastern teaching figure who personifies the folk hero portrayed as a 'wise idiot'. In one of the stories about him, he was sitting in the main street of his village fishing. The hook on the line of his fishing rod was hanging into a large pot of water standing in front of him.

A self-satisfied scholar passing by called out: 'Have you caught many today, you idiot?'

'Not many, your excellency, only three!'

'Three! Is that all?' smiled the self-appointed 'wise' man.

'Well, actually, you're right. It is four, including you,' replied Nasrudin.

Of course, it is a very good thing to be self-confident and to believe in yourself, but having wisdom also implies that you possess a solid dose of humility. In fact, among the many qualities that have been ascribed to wisdom, it is humility that really stands out. It is a quality that tends to make you more self-reflective. The power of humility forces you to realize how little you really understand about life, yourself and your surrounding world.

Clearly, wise people do not shout from the rooftops that they are wise. As the Roman statesman Cicero said, 'The higher we are placed, the more humbly we should walk.' What I am trying to say is that wisdom tends to be a very modest companion. At the same time, being humble does not mean that you are a nobody, that you have no qualities. Actually, if you are prepared to admit your weaknesses – including not knowing – it could be seen as a great sign of strength. It suggests that you are more open to the ideas of others, that you are willing to continue learning. After all –

returning to the story of the Zen master and the prospective student – if you think you know it all, how can you ever learn anything? Instead, you tend to remain stuck wherever you are. Thus, humility is a real doorway to true learning and personal growth.

However, although wise people may come across as being humble, they also do possess a solid dose of self-confidence. It is exactly the reason why they do not feel the need to show off. They are confident in what they stand for. They know what they are all about. Conversely, people who seem to be full of themselves, often, deep down, prove to be highly insecure. In fact, to behave like a show-off may reveal that, in reality, you know very little. If you behave this way, you had better remind yourself to focus on making yourself better, not on thinking that you are better.

If you remain humble about what you know, your search for wisdom will be a never-ending quest. You will recognize that continuous improvement is what really matters. In addition, you are more willing to learn from your mistakes. As a matter of fact, you have come to realize that the best thing about making the wrong decisions is that they do not prevent you from making the right decisions later on. As Mahatma Gandhi once said, 'It is unwise to be too sure of one's own wisdom. It is healthy to be reminded that the strongest might weaken and the wisest might err.' Thus, as I am suggesting, in most instances, your past failures and frustrations could lay the foundation for a deeper understanding of what is really important in life. Failure will always be a great educator, but only if you are prepared to learn from these experiences.

People who are presumably wise seem to have learned more from their failures than from their successes. They are prepared to acknowledge their mistakes. They own up to the fact that they may have been wrong. This is what humility is all about. Thus, in your search for wisdom, you would do well to always fight the specter of arrogance – it being the true enemy of humility. Like it or not, the mere fact of being human implies that this specter is always hovering about. Hubris will always be around the corner. All too easily, people who possess only a little bit of knowledge can become full of themselves. To maintain your narcissistic equilibrium will always be a delicate dance.

Over and over again, we can see how hubristic individuals are overestimating their abilities, their knowledge and their importance. Not surprisingly, like Icarus of Greek mythology, they might fly too close to the sun, melting their wings and then crashing down to earth. Furthermore, their tendency to overreach themselves – to take risky and reckless decisions – may also result in harmful, sometimes catastrophic, results for themselves, others, their organizations, institutions and even for society. Frankly speaking, hubris blinds people. It prevents them from seeing. It prevents them from acquiring a deeper understanding of things. Certainly, it blocks learning. In other words, too much ego is like cyanide. It is poisonous and is not a prescription for wisdom.

As there are so many unknowns, we may now have a better understanding of Socrates' humble response when asked about wisdom. Also, as the famous Russian writer Leo Tolstoy said many centuries afterwards, 'We can know only that we know nothing. And that is the highest degree of human wisdom.' In other words, if you are striving for wisdom, you have to continue to be an explorer; you have to continue to discover new things, and while you are on this exploratory journey, you should never be satisfied with where you are. You know that you will never know it all, making it very clear that arrogance has no place in the wisdom equation. For when arrogance is present, making good judgements becomes all the more challenging, which is another important aspect of the wisdom equation.

Good judgement

While living your life, you will have acquired your own values, beliefs and specific attitudes. You will have your own unique way of looking at the world. You will be seeing things through your own particular lens, but sadly enough, most people like to see what they want to see. You may even make the mistake of assuming that others see things exactly the way you do. However, when looking at life in this particular way, you may forget that nobody thinks alike. All of us will have our own set point of view, our own limitations in seeing. We are inclined to only discern the parts. To be able to see the whole is continually a challenge. Actually, the simple realization that there are other points of view may be the beginning of wisdom.

During your developmental journey, you will have formed prejudices and stereotypes about whatever, and whoever, you encounter. Usually, it is your close family members, your teachers and other people who touch you. They influence the way you interpret your world. Helped by these developmental experiences, you may have internalized their biases. You may have become selective in your perceptions and even more so in your emotional responses to whatever you see. Given the lenses you are using, you pass judgement upon things that are coming your way. Furthermore, depending on your specific biases, you may not so easily change your mind. You may hold on to your past judgements and preconceptions. Unfortunately, it is exactly these biases that contribute to closed-mindedness and contribute to an inaccurate perception of reality.

Thus, given these various psychological dynamics, you should remind yourself that your judgements about other people often say more about your own character than the character of the people you are pointing a finger at. You may have discovered, however, that the more you look into and understand yourself, the less judgemental you seem to become vis-à-vis others. In addition, whatever judgements you may have tend to be based on greater considerations. Fortunately, having better judgement indicates that you have become somewhat wiser.

Having good judgement will often also imply going against what are the established practices – not following prevailing rules and norms. Thus, good judgement implies critical thinking, thinking things through and not jumping to conclusions. In addition, good judgement pertains to the ability to make decisions based on the combination of knowledge, experience and an intuitive, deep understanding. Naturally, good judgement, as I am suggesting, will be an essential quality of the wisdom equation.

As wise people have a mind of their own, they tend to do what they think is right, not follow the crowd. Moreover, they view their mistakes as another, albeit difficult, learning opportunity. Perhaps, it is fair to say that having wisdom can derive from reflecting on bad judgement, thereby contributing to good judgement.

The Judgement of Solomon, a story in the first Book of Kings in the Bible, tells how King Solomon had to pass judgement in a case concerning two women who lived in the same house and had given birth at the same time. One of the children died shortly after its birth. Afterwards, both women claimed the living child as their own. Due to the conflict between them, they came to King Solomon to pass judgement. His wisdom led him to have a sword brought into the visitor's hall and to order the living child cloven in two so that each woman could have part of the child. With this strategy, Solomon was able to discern that the woman who approved of this cruel proposal was not the mother; while the actual mother begged that the sword be taken away and the child committed to the care of her rival.

As I have suggested before, nobody is born with wisdom. It comes from sound judgement, from a deep understanding of what makes the world go around. As I have emphasized, acquiring wisdom will always be a lifelong learning experience that starts when we are very young. It is very much related to how we grow up as responsible citizens – what developmental stages we pass through and what life experiences we have had. In the wisdom gathered over time, every new experience will be a form of exploration. It will be a journey that is never ending.

These insights on the development of wisdom are related to the work of the psychologists Jean Piaget and Lawrence Kohlberg, who suggested that the final stage of human moral development consists of complex moral reasoning, which should be the primary aim of character-building strategies.[1] This stage includes the ability to differentiate between right

[1] Jean Piaget (1965). *The Moral Judgment of the Child*. New York, NY: The Free Press; Lawrence Kohlberg and Richard Hersh (1977). Moral development: A review of the theory. *Theory into Practice*, 16 (2), 53–59.

and wrong in situations where we are without clear guidelines, as well as situations where different values may collide. It requires critical, ethical thinking. It also implies having empathy, the ability to put ourselves in other people's shoes.

Therefore, to reiterate, good judgement should be considered one of the major elements of the wisdom equation. Actually, wisdom and good judgement are semantically related. In some cases, we can even substitute the word 'wisdom' for 'good judgement'. It must now have become clear that good judgement includes considering the consequences of your decisions, thinking before acting and speaking, and having the tools to make good decisions in a variety of situations. As Francois Duc de la Rochefoucauld said, 'We sometimes see a fool possessed of talent, but never judgement.'

Obviously, there is a great difference between being judgemental and good judgement. The fact is that we have all been guilty of being judgemental at one time or another. In behaving in this way, however, you should always remember that when you judge someone, you are also judging yourself. You may be engaged in an exercise in mirroring, looking at yourself through the other. The question will be how you will interpret these reflections. Here, you should keep in mind that curved mirrors, like the ones seen at carnivals, can have strange, distorted effects.

Wise people never rush to judgement without examining all the evidence. They know how to apply relevant knowledge in an insightful manner, especially to different situations from that in which the knowledge was gained. One of the strengths of good judgement is that it can function as a corrective measure that counteracts faulty thinking, such as the tendency to favor one's current views or favoring ideas that are considered the dominant view. Furthermore, good judgement counteracts biased thinking, contributing to a more accurate decision-making process. In addition, individuals with the capacity of good judgement are less swayed by singular events and are more resistant to suggestions and manipulations. Good judgement implies also knowing what they have to accept, that there will be times when they have to face the reality of whatever dilemma comes their way. This is because when they can see things from more than one perspective, they will be more skilled in dealing with times of change and transition.

Given the possible effects of your actions, you may want to keep in mind the saying that often a moment of consideration can prevent a thousand apologies. In today's increasingly complex world, it is important to remember that leaders with good judgement will be the ones that stand out. They will be regarded as wise. Exercising good judgement will not only affect your attitudes and actions, but will guard you from the foolishness of the world. Ironically, as I have suggested before, good judgement comes from experience and experience comes from bad judgement.

Empathy and compassion

Having good judgement brings me to other important qualities found in the wisdom equation: empathy and compassion. In the pursuit of wisdom, empathy and compassion will stand out as being extremely important. When compassion and empathy are absent, it is most likely that wisdom will also be missing.

What should also be kept in mind – given the similarities between these two emotional reactions – is that compassion can be considered as the emotional response that creates the desire to be helpful, while empathy is an emotional attempt to understand how the other person feels. Although, as we are all different, we will never really know what it feels like to be in another person's shoes, we can at least try to imagine what another person's pain is all about. Empathy nurtures wisdom. Apathy cultivates ignorance. Thus, an important aspect of the wisdom equation is not only to reach out to others but also to try to put yourself into the shoes of others.

In more than one way, action without compassion and empathy is like planting a dead tree. However, if you do so, it will end up being a tree that never grows. Conversely, any action that contains compassion and empathy will be like planting a living tree that will keep on growing. Therefore, I am suggesting that whoever is full of wisdom will also be compassionate and such a person will also possess empathy. Let us consider this tale of two women and see what it has to tell us.

Two women, both seriously ill, were staying in the same hospital room. The woman who had the bed at the only window in the room was allowed to sit up part of the day to stretch her muscles. The other woman was in such a poor condition that she could only remain lying flat. Each day, the two women had very intense conversations talking about the men in their lives, their children, their jobs and the adventurous things they had done.

Every morning, when the woman in the bed by the window could sit up, she would describe to her neighbor what she was seeing outside her window. She would describe the people walking in the park and on the sidewalks. She would point out the flowering trees. She would describe the people sitting at the cafes. She would talk about the young lovers passing by. She would describe the ducks and swans swimming in the pond that were in the park. She would talk about the people that were feeding the pigeons. She would point out the cars that were passing by. At times, she would mention a Sunday parade with a very colourful musical band, describing in great detail how the band members were dressed. She would also talk about many other incidents happening outside the window. All in all, she would describe all the colorful events that were happening outside her window.

These short hours became very important to her roommate. It really made her feel more alive. Every time, she would be energized hearing about all these activities just outside the window. Naturally, the activities that were described made for very lively discussions and as the woman by the window described what was happening in such great detail, her neighbour was imagining all these scenes.

One morning, when the nurse arrived to clean the sheets and give the women their daily wash, she discovered that, during the night, the woman at the window had died. The other woman was overcome with sadness upon hearing the news. After the attendants took the body away, she asked if she could be moved to the bed next to the window. The nurse was happy to make the switch and, after making sure she was comfortable, she left her alone. Slowly, and very painfully, the woman managed to prop herself up on one elbow to take her first look at the world outside. Finally, she would have the joy of seeing for herself the world that had been described so many times to her. She strained as she slowly turned to look out the window beside the bed.

However, she was taken aback to discover that the window was facing a blank wall. The woman asked the nurse what could have compelled her deceased roommate to describe all these wonderful things happening outside this window. The nurse responded that the woman was blind and could not even see the wall. She said, 'Perhaps she just wanted to help you feel better.'

To reiterate, wisdom comes with a sense of humility, judgement, compassion and empathy. Due to these qualities, wise people will have a deep understanding of what really matters in life. Also, it may explain why these individuals, more likely, are able to make better decisions. Wise people strive for what is right and for what they think will be in everybody's best interest. Of course, as everyone's experiences are objectively and subjectively different, wisdom can manifest itself in many different ways.

Taking action: the ability to do what is right

Having an integrated humane view of what life is all about is just the beginning. As you may have observed in real life, wisdom also involves deeds that follow judgement, activities that will embody these integrated ideas of looking at life, while at the same time remaining compassionate and empathic. 'Knowledge is of no value unless you put it into practice,' to quote the Russian writer Anton Chekhov. Wisdom becomes the right use of knowledge. Thus, embodiment – actions taken to embody these integrated views in real-life situations – will be an essential part of the wisdom equation. After all, you can have many great ideas in your head, but what makes the real difference between fantasy and reality is action. It has often been said that vision without action is a hallucination.

Wisdom refers to doings things that we think are right. In that respect, as I must have made quite clear by now, as wisdom is inherently concerned with ethical and moral conduct, social justice will also be part of the proposition. Hence, part of the wisdom equation is to positively influence others at an individual, familial, communal, societal or even global level. When people are viewed as wise it is because they have been able to apply their wisdom in a way that benefits others. In contrast, people are seldom credited with wisdom when their actions only benefit themselves.

Furthermore, as we saw in the tale of the wise woman and the traveller, wisdom is not reserved for extraordinary souls. Both the renowned and the ordinary can display wisdom. Everyone who strives to live a meaningful and satisfying life can show wisdom. Clearly, many very ordinary people have displayed wisdom, even though many episodes of their wisdom will remain unknown to us. Just remember that people like Confucius, Buddha, Mahatma Gandhi, Nelson Mandela and Mother Teresa initially were not known for their wisdom. It took a considerable amount of time before they became better at sense making. They were only credited with wisdom after their endeavours generated positive effects towards others. Moreover, it took much time before they came to know what path would be the right one and what action would be most appropriate. Let us pause now and consider another tale.

An old man, a boy and a donkey were going to town. The boy rode on the donkey and the old man was walking. As they were going along, they passed some people who remarked that it was not right that the old man was walking and the boy was riding the donkey. The old man and boy thought maybe these critics had a point, so they changed positions.

A little later, they passed some other people who remarked, 'What a shame, the old man makes that little boy walk. Why isn't the boy on the donkey?' Once more, they decided there was some truth in that statement. To accommodate these critics, they decided that they both should walk.

Soon they passed some other people who thought that they were stupid to walk when they had this sturdy donkey to ride on. Their commentary made them decide that they would both ride on the donkey. Again they were criticized. While on the road, they met a number of people who shamed them by saying how horrible it was to put such a heavy burden on the poor donkey.

The boy and the man figured out that these people were probably right. They came to the decision to carry the donkey. As they crossed the bridge, they lost their grip on the animal. The old man, the boy and the donkey fell into the river and they all drowned.

Obviously, the moral of this story is that you should not let the expectations and opinions of other people take over your life and not let the behaviour of others destroy your inner peace. It is important that you figure out for yourself what feels right to you and what action you should be taking. Authenticity in whatever you are doing will be important. Of course, this does not mean that you should ignore what others are saying. In the end, however, the opinions of others are not what is important, but rather your own opinion about yourself in doing what you think is right. In other words, you should never judge yourself only through someone else's eyes. After all, it is your life, not theirs. You should do what matters most to you; you should do what you think feels right; you should do what makes you feel alive and happy. Always remember that if you let others tell you who you are, you are living their reality – not your own. Thus, keeping the story of the donkey in mind, there is more to life than pleasing other people and there is much more to life than following the prescribed paths of others.

What should have become clear by now is that the primary difference between wisdom and being knowledgeable or being intelligent is that with wisdom comes the realization of not knowing and a kind of humility – accompanied by a wish to always learn more. Furthermore, as I am suggesting, wisdom involves having a healthy dose of perspective, possessing the ability to make good judgements about the issues that you are dealing with. Wisdom will be associated with compassion and empathy. In addition, as I have mentioned before, wisdom will also have an action orientation – the consequences of actions are taken into consideration. After all, you should do something with the wisdom that you have acquired. Wisdom by its nature necessitates taking the kinds of actions that will have a moral component. The essence of wisdom is to know when to be taking action, and when it is useless even to try. Donkey owners had better be aware!

There will also be times – continuing this discussion of the wisdom equation – that the test of good judgement is to withhold your judgement, as the example of the farmer illustrates or as the psychologist William James once said, 'The art of being wise is knowing what to overlook.' Wise people have learned how to determine the truth and the validity of the knowledge that they have accumulated. They know when to act and when not to act. They also know how to be patient. In that respect, they have learned about the importance of timing. Therefore, a wise person is not just a person who knows things or is intelligent, but very much a person whose actions portray his or her wisdom. As I have indicated, within the leadership equation, there is no wisdom without many scars. It is a sign of having acquired experience. Wise leaders are not wise because they make no mistakes. They are wise because they correct their mistakes when they recognize them.

Given these reflections on wisdom, where do you think you are on the wisdom equation? Is humility one of your characteristics? Do you think you have good judgement? What about the qualities of compassion and empathy? Do you use these qualities to take considered action? Furthermore, when taking action, are you considering the ethical implications? In that respect, do you live your values? Reflecting seriously on these questions is critical to wise leadership. Perhaps there is merit then in pausing from time to time to consider how well you are applying these aspects of the wisdom equation.

3

Wisdom and sorrow

Small sorrows are talkative. Deep sorrows are silent.

—Seneca

Those who do not weep, do not see.

—Victor Hugo

Wisdom and sorrow

What should be very clear by now is that wisdom will always be a very elusive concept. In that respect, the pursuit of wisdom could be compared to a Sisyphean task. Relegated to forever roll a boulder up a hill in the depths of Hades, only to have it roll back down, Sisyphus was given a task that would never come to an end, and so too it is with seeking wisdom. The pursuit of wisdom should also be seen as an interminable challenge. However, unlike Sisyphus, wise people are in a position to learn something from their suffering and seek to do so. Perhaps, if they would be assigned

Sisyphus' task of rolling this boulder up the hill, they would welcome the boulder rolling down, considering it a brief opportunity for reflection.

In the wisdom equation, suffering can turn into one of life's great teachers. Suffering may help you find your inner strengths and hidden talents. Suffering can contribute to profound insights. Furthermore, having gone through difficult experiences could make you less judgemental. Hopefully, it also contributes to a more nuanced way of looking at things. Ironically, personal misfortunes may well lead you to a greater sense of compassion and empathy. Not only could these experiences give you a greater understanding of your own challenges, but also about other people's tribulations. This observation was already made in the Old Testament where it says: 'No sorrow, no wisdom.' Is it often true that tragedy tends to be the nursemaid of wisdom? Let us again take a pause and reflect on a famous story from Buddhism.

A woman by the name of Kisa Gotami, the wife of a wealthy man, lived during the days of the Buddha. A tragedy occurred and she lost her only child to death, which left her inconsolable. Unwilling to accept the lost, she carried her dead son from neighbor to neighbor, begging for medicine that would bring him back to life. One of her neighbors told her to go to the Buddha and ask him if he had a way to bring her son back to life. Encouraged by this advice, she went to the Buddha and asked, 'What prayers, what magical incantations do you have to bring my son back to life?'

Instead of sending her away or trying to reason with her, the Buddha said to her, 'Fetch me a mustard seed from a home that has never known sorrow. We will use it to drive the sorrow out of your life.' The woman felt a sense of relief. Soon after, she went off in search for this magical mustard seed.

She came first to a large mansion, knocked at the door, and said, 'I am looking for a home that has never known sorrow. If so, I would like to ask you for one of your mustard seeds. Is this such a place? It's very important to me.'

The owners told her, 'You've certainly come to the wrong place,' and began to describe all the tragic things that had happened to them. Very touched, Kisa left, but continued her search, going from house to house, from village to village, from town to town. But everywhere she went, visiting the rich and the poor, she would get the same answer. In spite of all her heroic efforts, she was still without any of the mustard seeds that she had been instructed to collect. It was impossible to find a home that had never known sorrow. Instead, wherever she turned, she was exposed to more tales of sadness and misfortune. Gradually, she understood that everyone had similar experiences as she had. It made her realize the universality of death.

Given what she had learned, Kisa said to herself, 'Who's better able to help these poor, unfortunate people than I, who have had misfortune of my own?'

Kisa's quest to find the magical mustard seed helped lessen her own suffering. She became so involved in helping others to cope with their sorrows that she eventually was able to let go of her own.

As you may have noted by now, knowledge comes from learning, wisdom comes from living. Clearly, wisdom is only learned through the tough school of experience – and that includes experiencing difficult times. However, as I have suggested before, acquiring wisdom will be a lifelong journey, and a never-ending one. While on this journey, the degree of wisdom you will be capable of achieving very much depends on how you deal with your life experiences – the degree to which you wisely use the knowledge that you have acquired.

Hopefully, the wisdom that comes your way will be something you can pass on to the next generation. Now let us consider the story of the farmer.

> *A farmer had become so old and frail that he could no longer work in the fields. He would spend the day just sitting on the porch thinking about his life experiences – telling his grandchildren some of the lessons he had learned in life. His son, still working the farm, would look up from time to time and see his father sitting there. 'He's of no use anymore,' the son thought to himself. 'He doesn't do anything anymore!' One day the son got so frustrated by his father's lack of apparent action that he built a wooden coffin, dragged it over to the porch and told his father to get in it. Without saying anything, the father climbed inside. After closing the lid, the son dragged the coffin to the edge of the farm where there was a very steep cliff. As he approached the edge, he heard a light tapping on the lid from inside the coffin. He opened it up. Still lying peacefully in the coffin, the father looked up at his son. 'I know you are going to throw me over the cliff, but before you do, may I suggest something?' 'What is it?' replied the son. 'Throw me over the cliff, if you like,' said the father, 'but save this good wood coffin. Eventually, your children might need one.'*

In this instance, the father taught his son a rather tragic lesson. Hopefully, it was an important learning experience for the son. In this case, ageing and wisdom came together. Unfortunately, however, just getting older is not necessarily a prescription for wisdom. To quote the Irish poet and playwright Oscar Wilde, 'With age comes wisdom, but sometimes age comes alone.' In fact, getting older is not necessarily an intellectually demanding process. Grey hair and wrinkles do not necessarily create wisdom. They are only a sign of ageing, not wisdom. After all, many of us have encountered old people who possess very little wisdom.

Hopefully, however, life has brought you wisdom through the wrong turns and missed opportunities you have encountered. As you may have discovered for yourself, sorrow can be a very harsh teacher, but if you are willing to reflect on these life experiences, wisdom can leap forward with huge steps. As the writer Marcel Proust once said, 'We don't receive wisdom; we must discover it for ourselves after a journey that no one can take for us or spare us.' Sometimes the hardest part of the journey is believing you are worthy of the trip. Like it or not, your life will always be a work in progress. In that respect, you could compare your life to a complex tapestry that is never completed. How to untangle the various threads of this work of art will be all up to you, but acquiring the ability to do this untangling can be a quite painful process. Your challenge is to learn from your wounds while taking this journey towards wisdom.

Know thyself

Perhaps, you are familiar with the following story. When I was a young man, I wanted to change the world, but I discovered that it was very difficult to change the world, so I tried to change my country. However, that also turned out to be an impossible task. When I found out that I could not change my country, I began to focus on my town. Again, I did not manage to change my town. Then, I tried to change my family. Again, like my other attempts at changing things, I failed. Now, as an old man, I realize the only thing I can do is to change myself. It made me realize that if long ago I had changed myself, I could have made an impact on my family. My family and I could have made an impact on my town. The town's impact could have changed my country and I could indeed have changed the world.

The moral of this story isn't difficult to guess. To quote once more the Persian poet Rūmī: 'Yesterday I was clever, so I wanted to change the world. Today I am wise, so I am changing myself.' However, it is not an easy task to engage in a journey of self-exploration. In fact, when one of the seven sages of ancient Greece, Thales of Miletus, was asked what he considered to be the most difficult thing in the world, he responded: 'Know thyself.' He realized that our biggest challenge in life is finding out what we really are all about, but he also understood that we have to understand ourselves before we can understand anything else. A measure of our wisdom is our ability to change.

All too often, you may have the fantasy that you know the minds of others while you hardly seem to know your own. You cherish the fantasy that you know what you are all about. However, this assumption may turn out to be only a mirage. Self-knowledge takes time, but it is self-knowledge that is the great power by which you will be able to comprehend and control your life. Thus, if you decide to embark on this journey towards self-knowledge, it will be one that can bring you very rich rewards. It could help you live a more complete life.

In other words, building a relationship with your inner self – in short, deciphering the various strands that are important to you – will help you to understand many things. It is self-knowledge that is the royal road to wisdom. This inscription was already inscribed at the entrance of the famous temple of Apollo in ancient Delphi. To acquire wisdom is all about a journey into the self and all about reflective thinking. This all points to the need for a journey of self-discovery– getting to know the scripts in your inner theatre – a journey that will require a receptivity to change. As the poet Rainer Maria Rilke once said, 'The only journey is the journey within.'

> *Said the monk, 'All these mountains and rivers and earth and stars – where do they come from?'*
> *Said the Zen Master, 'Where does your question come from? Search within!'*

However, in order for you to understand what you are all about – to search within to face your true self – you will need to be prepared to be vulnerable. If you are not prepared to show vulnerability, it will be impossible to explore your inner theatre – to find out the 'scripts' that drive you. You need to decipher these scripts, to understand the mystery that is you. After all, you need to bring to your conscious mind thoughts and feelings that are buried deeply within. You need to bring to the surface and examine repressed experiences and emotions, often originating in childhood. This kind of understanding will help you to set yourself free. It is the way to unblock your mental blocks. You should not let your mental blocks control you. While such a journey into the self may be uncomfortable, it is the only way to free yourself from the bonds of past experiences. It is the way to live more fully in the present.

To put it simply, to have a fulfilling life – to be able to love, work and play – you need to liberate yourself from your mental inhibitions. You need to develop a deep level of self-understanding of why you do what you do, which will in turn increase your personal growth. However, to embark on such a journey into the self requires acquiring insights – emotionally and cognitively – of the internal motivators that drive your thoughts, feelings and behaviors. Hopefully, however, the insights that emerge from this inner journey will help you to overcome dysfunctional behavior patterns.

The divided self

If you are prepared to look deeply at the mirror that is you, will you begin to see your true self? I am referring to a sense of self based on spontaneous authentic experiences – the feelings of being truly alive.[1] It is not until you can integrate your shadow side with the other parts of yourself to match your life's blueprint that you will be able to understand why so many things in the past did not work. However, to be able to reach that point – to go beyond this defensive façade that can be called your false self – necessitates that you identify your defensive armor. I am referring to the armor you believe you need to put on to be able to cope with life's vicissitudes. Once you begin to understand the make-up of this armor, you will start to be able to ask yourself whether all this armor is really necessary. Do you need all these defences? Is it possible to do with less? Can you try to be more, just you? What would it be like to be more authentic? Is it necessary to have a divided self? Would you be able to integrate the various parts of what is you?

To be able to be just you should be seen as a sign of genuine strength and courage. If not, just remind yourself that even though you may look well-adjusted being dressed in all

[1] Donald W. Winnicott (1960). Ego distortion in terms of true and false self. *The Maturational Process and the Facilitating Environment: Studies in the Theory of Emotional Development*. New York: International Universities Press, Inc., pp. 140–157.

this armor, all it does is to mask your insecurities and fears. Thus, in your search for what you are all about, you should be able to ask yourself: 'Do I dare to show more of my true self?' 'Do I dare to be vulnerable?' If you are willing to go down this road, it would be good to remind yourself that vulnerability really means to be strong and secure enough within yourself to show yourself without your defences. In fact, to be vulnerable should not be seen as a weakness. It is a true sign of strength. Although putting on a suit of armor may make you look tough, all it does is mask insecurity and fear. In contrast, to share your weaknesses means making yourself vulnerable and to make yourself vulnerable is showing your strength.

Naturally, this journey into the self also implies a confrontation with the darker parts of yourself – the demons that live inside you. Thus, during these encounters, you had better remind yourself not to put the qualities that you do not like about yourself into boxes and then become fearful of opening the lids. Like it or not, even the most seemingly adjusted among us have blind spots, and even the most honorable people may have a shadow side – a side that they may not know and may not even want to know. As I always say, 'Everybody is normal until you know them better.' Instead, you should accept that your shadow side will also be an important part of you. Even if it remains hidden, these darker and negative sides are part of your identity. If you ignore these parts of yourself, in your journey through life, you may end up in the wrong destination. Running away from these parts of yourself will be a race that you will never win.

You should keep in mind that certain adverse conditions, especially those that undermine your sense of control and security, can trigger the appearance of your shadow side. Therefore, you would be wise to learn what this darker side contains. If not, whatever you are all about stays divided. Also, keep in mind that living with such a divided self could cause many problems and does not make for authentic behavior. Here, I am referring to the tension between the two personas that may live within you: one, your authentic, more private identity (your true self), and the other, the false, supposedly, sane self that you are presenting to the world.[2]

Like it or not, if you are afraid to deal with the things you do not want to see, this darker side of yourself will reappear at the most undesirable moments, often without you even being fully aware of it. Therefore, instead of taking the route of repression – if you are prepared to undertake this journey within – prepare yourself to begin opening up these boxes. You have to look at what is inside and deal with it. You should be prepared to face all the pain, joy, irony and mystery that is part of being human.

When feeling blue, remind yourself that bad things happen to everyone. As the popular saying goes, life is not a rose garden. We all have our crosses to bear. The question will be how you are able to deal with it. Always keep in mind that there is nothing in this life that can really destroy you but yourself. However, if you have attained a degree of wisdom, you will manage to deal with the difficult issues that come your way. You will not be controlled by your mental blocks. Instead, you will try to transform these mental blocks into some kind of building blocks – to aim for future personal

---

[2] Ronald D. Laing (1990). *The Divided Self: An Existential Study in Sanity and Madness*. London: Penguin.

growth. Of course, doing so implies enduring the sharp pains of self-discovery rather than choosing to accept the dull pain of unawareness. You should remind yourself that it is the latter pain that does not go away. If you face your demons head-on, you will learn from experience. It is the road to further growth and transformation.

Self-development

As I must have made clear by now, to acquire wisdom comes with the desire for self-development. I am not just referring to cognitive processes, but especially to emotional ones. To continue to grow, you will need to become more astute in your emotional management. The ability to express emotions will be very important, but as you may have discovered by now, any emotional excess is bound to stir up trouble. Too much of it will be like smoke getting into your eyes. If you do not blow this smoke away, it will be difficult to see what is really going on. Without emotional astuteness, it will be hard to acquire night vision – that is, to see what is happening under the surface. Without night vision, it will be difficult to make wise decisions. Here again we will turn to a story to further our awareness.

> *There once was a boy with a very bad temper. His mother – being at her wits end – gave him a bag of nails and told him that every time he lost his temper, he needed to hammer a nail into a fence-post. The first day the boy ended up driving forty nails into the fence. As the wood was quite hard, hammering them all in required a considerable effort. Over the next few weeks as he learned to control his anger, the number of nails hammered in daily began to*

decrease gradually. He discovered it was much easier to hold his temper than to hammer those nails into the fencepost.

Eventually, the day came when the boy didn't lose his temper at all. No nails were driven into the fencepost. Proudly, he rushed over to his mother to tell her about this achievement. His mother was very pleased but suggested that he now pull out one nail for each day that he was able to hold his temper. Eventually, the day arrived when the boy was finally able to tell his mother that all the nails were gone.

The mother took her son by the hand and led him to the fence. She said, 'I am very proud of you. You have done very well. But look at the holes in the fence. This fence will never be the same. Always remember that when you say things in anger, these words will leave a scar just like these holes in the fence. Thus, after you insult someone, it won't matter how many times you say I'm sorry, but the wound will still be there. Thus, make sure you control your temper the next time you are tempted to say something that you will regret later.'

To become the producer, director and actor in the unfolding story that is your life is always a challenge. Moreover, making sense of what you are all about is going to take time. Furthermore, it will take patience. Thus, when taking this journey into your interior, you need to understand and accept the fact that sometimes things must unfold in their own time. That is important if you desire to be the architect of your own life. What is more, there are going to be times – and this may sound quite paradoxical – when you may have to lose yourself to be able to find yourself. Most often, however, only after you have stepped out of your comfort zone will you begin to change, grow and transform. Remember, a butterfly does not return to be a caterpillar after it is mature. On the contrary, it has gone through a dramatic transformation. Afterwards, it will never be the same. Like a butterfly, you must learn to grow and evolve into a stronger, wiser and better version of yourself. Life occurs in stages and taking one step at a time will be the key to learning, growing and maturing. All these transformations will require patience. Let us consider what the Buddha has to tell us about this.

> *Once the Buddha was walking from one town to another town with a few of his followers. While they were travelling, they happened to pass a lake. They stopped there and the Buddha told one of his disciples, 'I am thirsty. Can you get me some water from the lake?'*
>
> *The disciple walked up to the lake. When he reached it, he noticed that some people were washing clothes in the water, and, right at that moment, a bullock cart was crossing the water. As a result, the water had become quite muddy. The disciple thought, 'I cannot bring this muddy water to the Buddha to drink.' So he returned and told the Buddha, 'The water in there is very muddy. I don't think it is fit to drink.'*
>
> *After about half an hour, again the Buddha asked the same disciple to go back to the lake and get him some water to drink. The disciple obediently went back to the lake. This time he found that the lake had absolutely clear water in it. The mud had settled down and the water above it looked very drinkable. So, he filled up a bowl and brought it to the Buddha.*
>
> *The Buddha looked at the water and then he looked up at the disciple and said, 'Do you realize what you did to make the water clean? You let it be. After some time, the mud settled down on its own and you got clear water. The same can be said about your mind. When it is disturbed, just let it be. Be patient. Give it a little time. It will settle down on its own. You don't have to put in any effort to calm it down. It will happen.'*

Patience is also a form of wisdom. It shows that we accept the fact that sometimes things must unfold in their own time.

In my own case, I have spent much time reflecting on the things I have learned from the executives I worked with, patiently going over their comments again and again to see what I might learn. In this context, I have paid attention to the words of wisdom they imparted to me – observations about living that have lingered on. My discussions with them also gave me the idea to write down the lessons of life that I have learned from them. What helped in summarizing these lessons of life was to ask them the question, what would they say if asked to give a graduation speech to the students at their old university? What would they like the next generation to know? What lessons of wisdom would be top of their minds? What would they say to their listeners to make them more effective leaders? These discussions and my reflections on them over these years have led me to write down the following eight lessons on wisdom, which I would like to share with the readers of this book.

4

The Golden Rule

What you do not want done to yourself, do not do to others.

—Confucius

Act only according to that maxim by which you can at the same time will that it should become a universal law.

—Immanuel Kant

Lesson 1: The Golden Rule

One day the Buddha was walking through a village. A very angry young man came up and began insulting him, hurling all kinds of rude words at him, intended to ridicule and demean him.

The Buddha didn't appear to be upset at all by these insults. Instead, he asked the young man, 'Tell me, if you buy a gift for someone, and that person does not take it, to whom does the gift belong?'

The young man was surprised to be asked such a strange question and answered, 'Of course, it would belong to me, because I bought the gift.'
The Buddha smiled and said, 'That is correct. And it is exactly the same with your anger. If you become angry with me and I don't get insulted, then the anger falls back onto you. You are then the only one who becomes unhappy, not me. All you are doing is hurting yourself.'

The Golden Rule suggests that you always treat people the way you would like to be treated yourself. In other words, what you do not want to be done to you, you should not do to others. It is precisely the rule's simplicity that makes it so important and powerful, so simple to understand and so easy to apply. In fact, the Golden Rule can be looked at as the basis for a society's moral code, even the foundation of the modern concept of human rights. The Golden Rule emphasizes that we all have the right to fair treatment. Similarly, all of us have a reciprocal responsibility to ensure justice for others. Thus, no wonder, given its simplicity, that it is a rule to be found in many of the world's religions, dating back as far as ancient Egypt.

Wisdom and living according to the Golden Rule, very much go together. Wise people realize that this rule incorporates – as I have already suggested in Chapter 2 – humility, judgement, compassion, empathy and action. With wisdom comes a good understanding of what causes another person to suffer. People who possess wisdom realize that whatever they do, it will affect others. They always remind themselves that what is sent out tends to return. Moreover, they keep in mind that if they do not deal fairly with the other person they are not only betraying that person they are also betraying themselves.

Even though living according to the Golden Rule may sound like common sense, sadly enough it tends not to be common. Many of the people you will meet in life do not live according to this rule. They seem to be disrespectful in their treatment of others and they fail to realize that respectful and kind treatment is a two-way street – that in good relationships there will always be a sense of mutuality. In contrast, people with a degree of wisdom have due regard for the feelings, wishes or rights of others. They look at expressions of respect and kindness as an interactive process whereby empathy and compassion play an important role. They realize that living according to the Golden Rule means taking into consideration other people's feelings.

Thus, if the Golden Rule is important to you, before you say something to someone else, always ask yourself how you would feel if that person would say the same thing to you. Think, how would you react? And while you are reflecting on my comment, keep in the back of your mind that the way you make others feel about yourself tells a lot about you. Again, don't do to others what you would blame others for doing to you. What is more, wise people will act in this way indiscriminately of the other person's importance. Thus, do things for people not because of who they are or what they can do in return, but because of who *you* are. Let us consider what this professor of philosophy has to teach us.

During his first month at the university, a professor of philosophy gave his students a small exam. Most of the students had no difficulty in answering the questions except the last one. It was the question, 'What is the name of the person who cleans the classrooms?' Surely, the students thought, this must be a joke. However, in fact, all of them had seen this woman on many occasions. They recalled that she was tall, dark-haired and in her early sixties but how would they know her name? Most of them handed in their paper but left the last question unanswered.

When the students left the class, one of them stayed behind. He asked the professor, 'Does the last question really count toward the grade for the exam?'

'Absolutely,' said the professor. 'In your life, you will meet many people. You should always remind yourself that everyone counts. All of them deserve your attention and respect, even if all you do is smile and say "hello".' The student never forgot this lesson of his philosophy professor.

The importance of being kind

Living according to the Golden Rule naturally incorporates kindness. Being kind is an intrinsic part of the Golden Rule and here you should keep in mind that there is no such thing as a small act of kindness. Every act of kindness can have a potential ripple effect. As the philosophy professor tried to point out to his student, be generous with your kindness. Much can be said about both the kindness to strangers and the kindness from strangers. In fact, I have always found that a good indicator of people's character is how they treat people they do not know. Another significant indicator is how they are treating people who are at a disadvantage. In fact, is it true that you are only what you are when nobody is looking? Thus, never feel so important as not to be able to think of others.

Kindness is a way of showing others that they really matter. Furthermore, kindness is not simply about doing something for someone else because they cannot do it, but more importantly it is about extending oneself to others because *you* can. Kindness begins with the understanding that as human beings we all go through difficult times. We all need help at one time or another. Thus, why not be helpful? Why not be kind? Conversely, why would you ever be tempted to do something like humiliate another person?

In encounters with others, why not remind yourself that you rise by lifting others, not by putting people down. In addition, you would also do well to remember that no act of kindness will ever be wasted. As you may have discovered, most people respond positively to kindness. In addition, being kind not only has a direct effect on others, but it can also have a very positive impact on yourself. In fact, being kind is good for your mental health. It makes you feel better.

Thus, your wisdom is reflected in the way you treat other people for whom kindness is not a given. It is like handing over a gift without any strings attached. For wise people, however, being kind will be a part of their DNA. They realize that no act of kindness, no matter how small, is ever wasted. For them, living according to the Golden Rule is not a sacrifice. On the contrary, recognizing the need for kindness is an essential part of the wisdom equation. It fuels the Golden Rule. A tale from the *Fables of Aesop* elucidates this further.

> *In one of the Fables of Aesop, a small mouse was caught by a lion. The mouse pleaded for his freedom. After giving the idea some thought, the King of the Beasts released the mouse, thinking it being unworthy and too small to eat. Later, however, the lion was caught in a man-made trap. The mouse happened to pass by. When he saw the lion's predicament, he chewed the netting that trapped the lion and freed the lion. When the lion asked the mouse why he bothered to help him, the mouse replied, 'I have discovered that an act of kindness is never wasted!'*

The wonderful thing is that it is so incredibly easy to be kind. Even though it could be looked at as a long-term investment, one would hope that genuine kindness has nothing calculative about it. Scheming should have no place when applying the Golden Rule. It is what being civil is all about. It is what brings us together as a community and society.

Your challenge will be to be kind out of selflessness – to do kind things to others without ulterior motives, to view it as a natural thing to do. That being said, I do realize that there will always be some people who do not trust the power of the Golden Rule. They think expressing love, compassion, respect or kindness could make them look weak and even naive. They may even fear that if they show this side of them, people may take advantage of them. However, having such a *Weltanschauung* will be extremely shortsighted. It can also make for a very stressful life. In the longer run, looking out just for number one may turn out to be a truly poor investment.

Actually, the best thing to do, when you are dealing with people who are offensive and irritating – who are not practicing the Golden Rule – is to try to look past such behavior. In fact, something must have happened to have them behave in this way. You could try to understand why they are doing what they are doing. Why are they acting so unkindly? For example, why are they tempted to humiliate other people? Quite often, when people are hurting others, it is because they are hurting themselves. This does not mean that you should try to explain it away, that you should try to justify and rationalize inappropriate behavior. The decision to set boundaries concerning certain behavioral patterns is part of being morally responsible. Still, in trying to understand why these people are doing what they are doing, you could also keep in mind the words of Carl Jung: 'Everything that irritates us about others can lead us to an understanding of ourselves.' It may give you additional insights about what is happening as we all have a tendency to project unwanted parts of ourselves on to the other. It is far too easy to deposit on the other aspects of our shadow side – to use the other as some kind of 'garbage can'.

If you are capable of looking beyond unkind behavior – if you are able to keep your cool – you may discover that you can accomplish by kindness what you often cannot do by force. Kindness, being an important part of the Golden Rule, tends to be a highly effective way to ease difficult relationships. In fact, kindness will get you much further than resorting to swearing, threatening or belittling whoever stands in your way. As a matter of fact, unexpected kindness can be looked at as the most powerful, least costly and most underrated agent of human change. I would also like to add that kindness can be contagious. Often, to quote Sophocles, 'Kindness is the begetter of kindness.' Practicing kindness could make for a different world. Thus, try to be kind to unkind people – they may need it the most.

In fact, in a rather convoluted psychological way, the Golden Rule can also be viewed as acting rather selfishly. It can be quite selfish to be unselfish. Numerous studies have pointed out that people feel good when they help others.[1] As the Chinese saying goes: 'If you want happiness for an hour, take a nap. If you want happiness for a day, go fishing. If you

[1] Stephen G. Post (2005). Altruism, happiness, and health: It's good to be good, *International Journal of Behavioral Medicine*, 12 (2), 205–213.

want happiness for a year, inherit a fortune. If you want happiness for a lifetime, help somebody.'

Taking a more evolutionary point of view, we all have an inborn capacity for aggression as well as compassion. How these predispositions will evolve as we grow up very much depends on the mindful choices made by individuals and families, and how it is expressed within the communities and culture in which we live. How we end up depends on the socialization processes to which we are exposed. The balance between compassion and aggression very much depends on the outcome of a complex interface between our psychological make-up, our family background and our cultural and socio-political history.

From an evolutionary point of view, we may even be programmed to help others as a means of furthering our survival. The ability to cooperate with each other may have provided our Paleolithic ancestors with more food, better protection and better childcare, which in turn improved reproductive success. Thus, cooperative behavior may be part of our DNA. Of course, all relationships do not turn out that way. Among *Homo sapiens*, acts of aggression have also been ever-present. There has always been conflict about the availability of scarce resources. Therefore, the balance between cooperative and competitive behavior has always been a fragile one. All too often, negative forces negate possible acts of kindness. It does not take much to create situations that pit in-groups against out-groups with all their aggressive ramifications. Just imagine how different our world would be if we all spoke to everyone with respect and kindness. It may be the most vital key to the riddle of how all human beings can live in peace with each other. As the statesman and writer Johann Wolfgang von Goethe once said, 'Kindness is the golden chain by which society is bound together.'

Coming back to the Golden Rule, it does not matter how much time you are spending on this earth of ours, how much money you have gathered or how much attention you have received. It is the positive ripples that you have spread around in life that really matter. After all, life is short. There is not much time to improve the lives of the people that you will encounter. Therefore, you cannot engage in an act of kindness too early, for you never know how soon it will be too late. Generally speaking, practicing the Golden Rule will make for a better life and a better world. Wise people are all too aware of this!

As you are now familiar with the Golden Rule, you should ask yourself every day whether you are practicing this rule. Are you acting respectfully towards others? Have you been kind to some people today? Are you making being kind part of your daily *modus operandi*? Is it part of your leadership style? Have you noticed the extent to which being kind has been changing your world? Given the importance of the Golden Rule, why not start practicing it now?

5

Forgiveness

Let us forgive each other, only then will we live in peace.

—Leo Tolstoy

The weak can never forgive. Forgiveness is the attribute of the strong.

—Mahatma Gandhi

Lesson 2: Forgiveness

Once upon a time, two brothers living on neighboring farms got into a fight. It was a disastrous fight as they stopped talking to each other. Before the fight, they had been farming together for many years, sharing their equipment and helping each other with the work on the farms when needed. Suddenly, however, due to a small misunderstanding, their relationship had fallen apart completely. Sadly enough, what had started as a small misjudgement grew into a major difference, resulting in very harsh words, and eventually an icy silence.

One morning, there was a knock on the door of the older brother's farm. He opened it to find an elderly man standing there with a carpenter's toolbox. 'I'm looking for a few days' work,' the carpenter said. 'Perhaps you would have a few small jobs I can work on at your farm.'

'Yes,' said the older brother. 'Do I have a job for you! Look across the creek at that farm. That's my neighbor. In fact, it's not just my neighbor, it's my younger brother. Last week there was a small meadow between the two farms. A few days ago, however, my brother took his bulldozer to the stream close by, dug a ditch and now he has created a creek between our two farms. He just did it to irritate me. But I know how I can get back at him. Do you see all that lumber next to the barn? I want you to build me a high fence, so that I don't have to look at his place any longer. That will show him!'

The carpenter said, 'Fine, no problem. I think I understand the situation. I will get at it right now.' When the carpenter went off to collect the wood for the fence, the older brother took his truck to go to town to do a number of errands.

The carpenter worked hard all that day measuring, sawing and nailing. In the evening when the farmer returned, the carpenter had just finished the work. When the farmer arrived, he couldn't believe his eyes. The carpenter hadn't built a fence at all. Instead, he had built a beautiful bridge that stretched from one side of the creek to the other. It was really a great piece of work that even included a handrail.

While the older brother was looking at the bridge, he saw his younger brother coming across it with his hand outstretched. 'You are amazing building this bridge after all the things I've said and done.' The two brothers stood at each end of the bridge and then they met in the middle, shaking each other's hand.

When they turned around, they saw that the carpenter was leaving. 'No, please wait,' the older brother said. 'Can't you stay a few days longer? I've a lot of other things for you to do. 'I'd love to stay,' the carpenter said, 'but I have so many more bridges to build.'

Building bridges

Actually, as this story points out, when you do not forgive, you break the bridge over which you can pass. When someone wrongs you and you wrong the person in retaliation, it does not make you right. Instead, it makes both of you wrong. As you may have realized, a large part of life consists of making choices. It is one of our major existential challenges. Being able to show forgiveness is a critical, liberating choice. In fact, it is the best gift that you can give to yourself. It is a gift that will stop your imprisonment. It is a gift that can bring you freedom.

As the opening tale of this chapter suggests, every day you have the choice between building fences or building bridges. One approach leads to isolation and irritation, the other to togetherness. Perhaps, next time, when somebody does you a wrong, you could remind yourself of all the things he or she did right. It might change your point of view. Even when whatever unfortunate thing happened was not your fault, the way you react to it will still be your responsibility. It is up to you to react wisely.

Therefore, what this anecdote points out quite clearly is to have a forgiving attitude is an integral part of the wisdom equation. To hang on to anger due to past mistakes, because of hurtful breakups, toxic family relationships or the presence of hurtful lies is not a good way to live. It does not help you to grow, develop and mature.

Actually, you may discover that there is an extraordinary healing power in taking steps to forgive somebody, and that includes yourself. Although forgiving someone will not necessarily change the other person, it might very well change you. Therefore, it is quite unfortunate, in spite of its many benefits, that forgiveness is still one of the hardest things to do in life. For many people, to forgive requires a deep inner struggle. For many, to have a forgiving attitude seems to be impossible, but if they are able to forgive, they no longer torment themselves. They are able to break free. Thus, each time you are caught in a situation that begs for forgiveness, it would be wise to remind yourself that you can get bitter or you can get better.

Fortunately, as we grow in wisdom, we will be more prepared to forgive. As a matter of fact, a true mark of wisdom is that, when you are hurt by someone, you try to understand why, instead of immediately going into overdrive and wanting to hurt back. Unfortunately, far too many people are more prone to revenge injuries than to resort to kindness. For many, the Lex Talionis (the law of the talon) has a place of pride, but as has been said many times over, an eye for an eye makes the whole world blind. Refraining from employing the Lex Talionis will take courage.

Refusing to engage the process of forgiveness can also have major mental health implications. A lack of forgiveness will evoke many negative emotions, such as envy, jealousy, disgust and anger, the impact of which can cause a great deal of harm. The damage to your mental and physical health can be significant. Moreover, when feelings of anger take over, wisdom tends to disappear. The Buddha said it very astutely: 'Holding on to anger is like grasping a hot coal with the intent of throwing it at someone else, but you will be the one that gets burned.' In fact, if you give the matter serious thought, resorting to anger is often far too easy a choice. It is too much of an instinctual response. Instead, to be able to control your impulse to lash out will be much more of a challenge. Sadly enough, if you resort to such a knee-jerk reaction, you could remind yourself that anger only spreads anger. As the writer Jane Austen said pointedly: 'Angry people are not always wise.'

Always keep in mind that forgiving means to make peace with your past so that you do not allow yourself to destroy your present and your future. In other words, remind yourself that forgiveness is not something you just do for other people. It is something that you do very much for yourself. Forgiveness helps you to move on. It also makes you feel better. If not, like any other unprocessed, difficult emotional experiences, they have a tendency – consciously or unconsciously – to linger on. They will clutter your mind and just repressing these feelings will not be the answer. Actually, being unable to forgive is like taking poison with the strange hope that the other person will die. Therefore, once you take a hard look at what comes with not forgiving, it becomes evident that being preoccupied with negative thoughts about someone else does not make any sense. It is a short-sighted way of going on with living. The following Zen story is quite explicit about the importance of letting things go.

An old monk and a young monk were travelling together. At one point, they came to a river with a strong current. As the monks were preparing to cross the river, they saw a very young and beautiful woman also attempting to cross. The young woman called out to them asking for help to cross the river as she feared its current.

The two monks glanced at one another because they had taken vows not to touch a woman.

Then, without a word, the older monk picked up the woman, carried her across the river and placed her gently on the other side. Then the young woman went on her way. The monks continued their walk to the monastery.

The young monk was shocked by what had just happened. After rejoining his companion, he was speechless. However, after a couple of hours the young monk could no longer contain himself and said: 'As monks we have vowed not to look or touch a woman, how could you carry that woman on your shoulders?'

The older monk looked at him and replied, 'Brother, a long time ago I set her down on the other side of the river, so why are you still carrying her?'

In fact, without forgiveness – if you act like the younger monk – you are likely to get stuck in an endless cycle of discontent. If you maintain your unforgiving attitude, you will always stay bound to the other person. Conversely, if you are able to forgive, it is like you are liberating yourself. You are setting yourself free. You can make new beginnings.

Of course, forgiving is never going to be easy. Forgiving is a process and processes will take time. In that respect, the ability to forgive should be looked at as the last stage of a grieving process. It should be looked at as the acceptance/detachment phase of this process of letting go, a stage when your emotions begin to stabilize, when you are re-entering reality after having gone through a stressful experience.[1] However, acceptance of what has happened does not mean

[1] John Bowlby (1983). *Attachment: Attachment and Loss*, Volume One. New York: Basic Books.

a happy ending. It means that you have come to grips with the situation and are able to move one. You reckon that what has happened has not been a 'good' thing, but you have now learned to live with it. In other words, adjustment and readjustment have taken its course. In addition, I should add that there can be a time element worth considering when it comes to forgiveness since you never know when it is going to be too late – when the person in question will no longer be alive. This is another good reason to choose the path of forgiveness.

Keep in mind that it is a very rare person who is completely wicked – just as no person is perfect. This is worth keeping in mind when someone really upsets you. Look for the good in every person and every situation. You will be surprised what you will find. What you should understand and accept is that there is no person, including yourself, without flaws; that you live in an imperfect world with imperfect people. Like it or not, finding perfection will always be a pipe dream. In fact, the best relationships are not the ones made up of perfect people. They are the ones whereby each individual learns to live with the imperfections of the other. I am referring to the capacity to appreciate the other person's good and bad qualities. To have a binary outlook towards the world, to see things in black and white, will never be the answer. Boring as it may sound, grey is a far more realistic colour.

What can actually contribute to one's misery is the search for perfection. As you may have discovered during your life's journey, we all make mistakes; we all have our limitations. All of us will be disappointed in others, including ourselves, but having a forgiving attitude is a good way to overcome these disappointments. The more you know yourself – and the wiser you may become – the more you will be inclined to forgive others. In that respect, forgiveness is also self-forgiveness and, most importantly, it is a much saner and wiser way to live. Let us consider the story of the two friends.

> *There were once two friends walking through a desert. At some point during their journey, they were having an intense argument. In a bout of anger, one of the friends slapped the other one in the face.*
>
> *The one who got slapped felt quite hurt, but without saying anything, he wrote in the sand: 'Today my best friend slapped me in the face.'*
>
> *The two friends kept on walking until they found an oasis, where they decided to take a swim, but the one who had been slapped in the face got stuck in quicksand and started to drown. Fortunately, his friend saw what was happening and managed to pull him out. After he recovered from his near drowning, he wrote on a stone: 'Today my best friend saved my life.'*
>
> *The friend who had slapped and saved his best friend life asked him: 'After I hurt you, you wrote in the sand and now, after saving your life, you write on a stone, why are you doing all this?'*
>
> *The other friend replied: 'When someone hurts you, you should write it down in loose sand where the winds of forgiveness can erase it. However, when someone does something good for you, you must engrave it in stone where no wind can ever erase it.'*

Not forgetting

Another way of looking at forgiveness is seeing it as a freedom from hatred. Hatred will always be a very strong emotion and, as you may have discovered, hatred is not good for you. Similar to other negative emotions, feelings of hatred can build up in the mind, body and soul, affecting the body's organs and natural processes and breeding even more negative emotions. Allowing hatred to continue to live inside you will take its toll on your body in the form of stress reactions such as high blood pressure, feelings of anxiety, headaches, stomach aches and poor circulation. It will eat you up inside. You may even give yourself a heart attack and, however difficult it is to acknowledge, you will be the one responsible. With wisdom, however, you may realize that to continue to hold grudges only creates bitterness and vindictiveness.

Thus, if you do not forgive, you may end up becoming a prisoner of your own hatred, with yourself functioning in the role of a prison guard, and you aren't doing yourself a favor. You are hurting yourself. Eventually, you may even be killing yourself and, while stuck in your own self-created prison of hatred, you may be doomed to repeat your mistakes over and over again. In that respect, forgiveness could be reframed as a reflection of loving yourself enough to move on, and while you are moving on, you should remind yourself that you are not necessarily approving of what has happened, but you have decided to rise above it. Thus, forgiving will not change the past, but it can enlarge the future. While you are not forgetting what has happened, you are trying to rise above it.

'Why do you keep talking about my past mistakes?' said the husband. 'I thought you had forgiven and forgotten.'

'I have, indeed,' said the wife. 'But don't you ever forget that I have forgiven and forgotten.'

I guess the wife did not pay heed to Confucius' admonition when he said, 'To be wronged is nothing, unless you continue to remember it.'

Of course, as I mentioned before, forgiving does not erase what has happened. In other words, forgiveness is not forgetting. After all, a healed memory is not a deleted memory, but, as I have said before, the challenge will be to reframe the experience. Thus, wise people learn from hurtful relationships, but they also keep in mind that forgiveness does not necessarily mean that they will have to deal in the future with the person that has hurt them. Most likely, a level of toxicity around the relationship will be lingering on. In that respect, forgiving may not always be the hardest part. It is being able to trust the other person again. Often, it will be quite difficult to rebuild trust after trust has been broken. In other words, you can forgive someone and still take a healthy approach to not wanting this person to be a part of your life in the future. Again, as I said before, with forgiveness, you can move on.

A virtue of the brave

Some people may think that forgiveness is weakness, but that is absolutely not the case. As India's late prime minister Indira Gandhi once said, 'Forgiveness is a virtue of the brave.' Conversely, it is the weak people who seek revenge. Actually, it is fair to say that the person who forgives is always stronger than the person who prefers to continue fighting. As I have made quite clear by now, not forgiving tends to be a dead end. Thus, how wrong people can be when they suggest that those people who forgive are weak.

The ability to forgive can be seen as a major contribution to the healing of the world. Once more, taking a hard look at this world of ours, it is for all to see that retaliation is not the answer. It only results in more strife and misery.

Unfortunately, however, for too many people, 'an eye for an eye' is still their favorite choice. People who act in this manner seem to be unable to go beyond rather instinctual responses. However, if we want to create better places to live – to create more humane societies – forgiveness is going to be the best revenge. Naturally, if we want to heal this complex, entangled world of ours, we had better start with ourselves. Self-healing comes from self-knowledge, but to be able to undertake such a journey will necessitate great wisdom.

Forgiveness, human decency and goodness are the forces that can move human affairs. Life is too short to hang on to animosity or keep on registering wrongs. While, as I have explained, forgiveness does not overlook whatever bad things have been done to you, it does require that you rise above them. In that respect, forgiveness is one of the most important first steps to ending conflicts in your families, your communities and between nations. It is an act of the imagination. It challenges you to give up your destructive thoughts about the situation and to believe in the possibility of a better future. In other words, forgiveness is a major force that will stop the disintegration of societies. To quote the Dalai Lama, 'While revenge weakens society, forgiveness gives it strength.' When you forgive, you in no way change the past, but you are sure to change the future.

To be able to forgive should be seen as a developmental challenge. Hopefully, you learn to forgive early in life. The way children can learn the habit of forgiveness is by seeing their parents forgive others and forgive themselves. In that respect, teaching the practice of forgiveness to the next generation can be a great contribution to the healing of the world. If this is not done, then you had better keep in mind the Chinese proverb: 'The man who opts for revenge should dig two graves.'

Thus, after these observations about forgiveness, ask yourself, do you find yourself in a situation with someone else that begs for forgiveness? Are you stuck in a difficult relationship? Could it be that forgiveness is needed not just on a personal level, but at a societal one? Has it become the source of serious inter-group conflict? If that is the case, are you willing to get out of your comfort zone, forgive and move on? Thus, why not start doing so today? Why not make a small contribution to the creation of a better world?

Envy

Do not overrate what you have received, or envy others. He who envies others doesn't obtain peace of mind.

—Buddha

The covetous man is always in want.

—Horace

Lesson 3: Envy

We all know the fairy tale about Cinderella and her stepsisters. Even though it seems like it had a happy ending, in reality, given what is happening, it is not a very happy tale. However, like with most fairy tales, we can draw lessons from it – an important lesson being how wretched human behavior can be. In fact, taking a hard look at the story, it is really the tale of two stepsisters who are full of envy. They are very envious of Cinderella's beauty. They are envious of her skills. They are envious of her peace of mind. These are some of the qualities that they seem to be lacking. Given the way they behave towards their stepsister, it is as if they feel

> *persecuted by all the good in her. And of course, to top off all these miserable feelings, we should not forget their envy vis-à-vis the prince. Probably, it is fair to say that not only do they want what Cinderella has, they also want her not to have what she could possibly get. They would like to spoil things for her. Cold and cruel as they seem to be, they are acting extremely spitefully and vindictively towards their stepsister. In fact, they appear to be doing anything in their power to annoy, hurt or upset Cinderella, believing that the qualities she possessed were beyond their power to obtain. Clearly, given the way they were acting, they were direly lacking in wisdom.*

Unfortunately, for some people, the need to derogate someone whom they envy, becomes all-consuming. Similar to Cinderella's sisters, they become vindictive and act spitefully. Sadly enough, by putting other people down, they are trying to lift themselves up. We can ask ourselves, however, whether that is a wise way of dealing with the challenges that life has to offer. Obviously, envy and wisdom are not compatible roommates.

Actually, there is no passion so strongly rooted in the human heart as envy, but even though it is ever-present, it remains a very embarrassing emotion, something that does not enhance our self-image.[1] It is not something we like to brag about. Unpleasant as it can be, however, it is an emotional force that lies at the core of our lives as social beings and comes to the fore as soon as two individuals are capable of mutual comparison. In fact, truth be told, envy is inherent in our nature, starting with the sibling and Oedipal rivalry

---

[1] Manfred F. R. Kets de Vries (1988), The motivating role of envy: A forgotten factor in management theory. *INSEAD Research papers*, 88/28.

that will be experienced among small children.[2] Clearly, small children can be extremely self-centered. At that early stage of life, each sibling wants to have full possession of the parent, a desire that can have negative repercussions. Unfortunately, this imagined state of paradise will always be unattainable.

Sadly enough, what starts as micro envy can have macro effects. It can have major socio-political implications. We can even go as far as saying, taking a social perspective, that it is envy that makes the world go round. Without envy, the interplay of social forces within society would be unthinkable. Some people even suggest that envy is the key driving force behind individual and social human progress, but also behind society's regress – meaning the growth of social and economic inequality. All in all, as human beings, we experience a great need to equalize. In fact, the tall poppy syndrome is alive and well, and very present in most societies. No wonder that we can get quite perturbed when someone else is better off than ourselves, making envy a common response to another person's advantage.

What also should be kept in mind is that wanting what another person possesses is not necessarily a bad thing. Envy can be a great motivating force. For example, you may need a degree of envy to have ambition. Being somewhat envious of another person may motivate you to work harder – to get to where you really want to be. Actually, due to envy, you may go down a successful path that you would have otherwise never taken. Hopefully, however, when you are caught by envious

---

[2] Sigmund Freud (1964). New Introductory Lectures on Psycho-analysis and Other Works, pp. 1–267. *The Standard Edition of the Complete Psychological Works of Sigmund Freud*, Volume XXII (1932–1936), James Strachey (ed.). London: The Hogarth Press and the Institute of Psycho-analysis.

feelings, they will be transformed into a stimulus to better yourself, not to spoil life for others.

In addition, the awareness of the potential envy of others, and the fear of arousing it, can become a powerful force from the perspective of social control.[3] Institutionally, it may determine how human society and human behavior are structured to protect us from the actions of envious people through the existence of property rights, legal systems and moral codes. Furthermore, given the salient role that envious feelings can play, societies also try to reduce our envy through progressive taxation, the creation of social taboos and the making of social justice.

Notwithstanding the fact that envy can be used as a positive force, like with so many other things in life, it is the excess that can become problematic. Excessive envy can exact serious economic penalties. For example, we can observe how the fear of other people's envy could discourage innovation, creative efforts and positive achievements. Of course, in this context, the question of what is excessive can be raised. Not surprisingly, excess can be hard to define. Generally speaking, however, I am referring to situations whereby the only purpose of envy is to thwart the efforts of others – that is when envy is transformed into a highly destructive force.

The darker side of envy

As envy is part of human nature, we will all have to deal with it and, as I mentioned before, the problem with envy

[3] Helmut Schoeck (1987). *Envy: A Theory of Social Behaviour*. Carmel, IN: Liberty Fund.

becomes most acute when the degree of envy is excessive, which is something that is not always easy to assess, as envy can manifest itself in so many different ways. Not only do envious people desire whatever someone else possesses (like wealth, power, status, love or beauty) but they also may want to become spoilers – acting spitefully against whoever possesses the things they would like to have. Thus, envy will always bring forth a kaleidoscope of emotional reactions. For example, feelings of frustration, self-pity, greed, spite and vindictiveness could come into play. When envy takes the upper hand, feelings of anger can also appear. This explains why envy is associated with so many instances of violence in human history.

Interestingly enough, envious people will often justify their aggressive feelings by rationalizing them, assuring themselves that the advantages of the people they envy are unfair. They will tell themselves that these people do not deserve whatever they have. Another path taken on this dark, envious road is that they devalue whatever is desired. If that is the case, sour grapes see the light of day. One of Aesop's fables is a good illustration of these complex, dark psychological dynamics.

One afternoon a fox was walking through the forest and spotted a bunch of grapes hanging from over a lofty branch. 'Just the thing to quench my thirst,' he thought. Taking a few steps back, the fox jumped and just missed the hanging grapes. Again, the fox took a few paces back and tried to reach the grapes but still failed. Finally, giving up, the fox turned up his nose and said, 'They're probably sour anyway,' and proceeded to walk away.

Sadly enough, people haunted by the force of envy are often completely blind to their own achievements. They seem to be too preoccupied in trying to get what another person has, but while doing so, they are incapable of recognizing their own capabilities. They do not appreciate what they themselves have to offer. It is as though they are being hypnotized by the person whom they envy, but while being ensnared by the dark force of envy, they create a negative force field around themselves – a state of mind not helpful to do the things they need to do themselves if they want to be successful. In fact, they are counting other people's blessings, not their own. Busy as they are in envying other people, they forget to focus on their own goals, but allowing themselves to engage in this kind of mindset is not helpful if they plan to engage in more positive, constructive activities. On the contrary, to be obsessed about finding ways to destroy the lives of others is not a very worthwhile way to move forward. Certainly, it is not a sign of wisdom. In the end, the only thing that these people accomplish is the perverse satisfaction that they may have destroyed other people's dreams.

Envy versus jealousy

I should add that we often tend to confuse envy with jealousy. In distinguishing between these two emotions, however, it should be noted that jealousy occurs when you worry that someone will take what you have. In comparison, envy is wanting what someone else possesses. Thus, jealousy occurs when something that you already have (in most instances, having to do with a special relationship) is threatened by a third person. Envy, on the other hand, happens when you lack a desired attribute that someone else possesses. In other words, envy is a two-person situation, whereas jealousy refers to a three-person situation. To be more precise, while envy has to do with lacking something, jealousy is a reaction to the threat of losing something (usually some person).

Of course, the reason for the confusion between these two feelings is that they tend to be quite similar, even though they are also very different. Semantically, however, the words 'envy' and 'jealousy' often tend to be used interchangeably. Furthermore, what adds to the confusion is that jealousy and envy often travel together. Both feelings can occur at the same time. You can be both jealous and envious of another person.

Moral indignation

The poet Wystan Hugh Auden once said in his poem, *The essence of creation*: 'That reason may not force us to commit, That sin of the high-minded, sublimation, That damns the soul by praising it.' Thus, what may have started as envy easily becomes transformed into moral indignation and outrage. These high-minded people make the accusation – while rationalizing their negativity – that the people who they envy are morally flawed. Generally speaking, however, the louder the condemnation, the greater the envious feelings that are hovering about. As can be observed over and over again, moral outrage is often extolled and enacted not with an eye to arrive at a positive outcome. On the contrary, all too often, while pretending to be defenders of morality, these people – in a very hypocritical way – are only advancing their own interests. Truth be spoken, while holding on to the belief of seeing themselves as upstanding and moral, these people behave in a manner quite inconsistent with such a belief.

It is worth noting again that if there is something that irritates us about others, often it teaches us something about ourselves. In other words, moral indignation says more about the people who pretend to be upset than the ones towards whom their venom is directed. Often they are projecting their own insecurities, flaws and weaknesses on to others. When these high-minded people strongly judge someone else, it could very well be that they are doing so in order to avoid confronting this shadow side in themselves. In reality, however, given the frequent mismatch between their judgements and their actions, these moral hypocrites – imprisoned as they are by their envious feelings – are undermining their claim to moral authority. Obviously, there is not much wisdom in such behavior.

Thus, be warned when your envy becomes all-consuming. If so, a degree of soul searching might be in order. It would be wise to realize that when you are caught in the thrall of envy, not only may you be hurting others, but you also may be hurting yourself. What is even worse is the fact that excessive envy does not make for a good life. Like other negative emotions, it can have serious mental and physical health repercussions. It is much wiser to enjoy what you have without feeling compelled to always make comparisons with the lives of others. As has been said many times over, doing well is the best revenge.

Feeling inferior

It seems to be apparent that many envious people may have self-esteem problems. They may suffer from feelings of inferiority. In fact, another way of looking at envy is to see it as a derivative of insecurity about these envious people's own gifts – not valuing what they possess themselves. In addition, what may further aggravate these envious feelings is the perceived self-confidence – at least in their imagination – of the people that they envy. The apparent overconfidence of these people seems to transform into a red flag, rubbing in their own sense of insecurity. However, while they are beating themselves up mentally – given how unflatteringly they compare themselves to others – they are often far of the mark. In reality, their object of envy may not be as glorious as they imagine. While going through these strange psychodynamic acrobatics, what they seem to be forgetting is that there will always be some people who will be better, smarter or stronger than they ever will be, but instead of finding peace with this reality, they remain focused on whomever or whatever they envy, turning their envious feelings into a highly destructive self-flagellation exercise.

It is a truism to say that if you possess a secure sense of self-esteem – if you recognize your own capabilities – you are less likely to be envious of others. Therefore, generally speaking, you would do well to remind yourself that you do not have to put others down to lift yourself up. To quote the Roman Stoic philosopher Seneca: 'What you think of yourself is much more important than what others think of you.' Always keep in mind that nobody can make you feel inferior without your own consent. How you feel about yourself will always be up to you. In that respect, self-confidence is forever an inside job. Clearly, to have your self-worth determined by others does not make for a life well lived and being caught up in a web of envy does not bring wisdom.

Beyond envy

Once there was a man at the market selling crayfish. He had placed the crayfish into two buckets: one was covered and the other one was uncovered. One buyer passed by asking the fisherman the difference between the crayfish in the two buckets. Were the crayfish of different quality? The salesman responded, 'not really.' When the buyer insisted, he said: 'Actually, there is a difference. The crayfish in the covered bucket come from the river; the ones in the uncovered bucket come from the lake.' He added, 'You see the crayfish from the river escape easily. When one of them tries to get out, the others push him up, until he gets out of the bucket. That is the reason I need to put a lid on it. On the other hand, the crayfish from the lake do the opposite. As soon as they see that one of them is trying to escape, they try to pull at him and push him down, so that he falls back to the bottom of the bucket. It seems that they do not want any one of them to succeed.'

So, what kind of crayfish would you like to be? Do you want to be the kind of crayfish that pulls others down or are you willing to push them up? Whatever choice you make, you should keep in mind that when caught in the web of envy, you are really poisoning your capacity to enjoy the good things in life. One thing that distinguishes the wise from the unwise is that they know how to keep their envious feelings within boundaries. They do not waste their time and energy comparing their life with the lives of others. Instead, they focus on what they have and who they can become.

Obviously, for people caught in the web of envy, compassion and empathy are alien concepts. Such feelings will have fallen by the wayside. However, in a leadership context, these are essential aspects of what reflective leadership is all about. All of us need to recognize that spoiling things for others is not good for ourselves, for others or for society, and it certainly does not make for wisdom. Perhaps, the time has come to take a hard look at yourself, asking yourself whether you may be a prisoner of envy. If so, what are you doing to free yourself and others from this imprisoning web?

7

Greed

This avarice,
Strikes deeper, grows with more pernicious root.

—William Shakespeare

It is preoccupation with possessions, more than anything else, that prevents us from living freely and nobly.

—Henry Thoreau

Lesson 4: Greed

While envy is a resentful emotion reflecting the need to possess a perceived superior quality, achievement or possession that someone else has, greed is an insatiable longing for wealth, status and power. Like envy, greed has to do with human beings' insecurities, so no wonder it has been with us forever. It is yet another dark side of human nature and has little to do with wisdom. In fact, wisdom and greed may be positioned at the opposite ends of a spectrum.

A wise man was passing through the capital city of a famous king. While he was walking, he noticed a diamond necklace lying on the road. He picked it up, but as he was satisfied with living a humble life, he had no use for the necklace so planned to give it to someone in need. However, as he strolled around the streets throughout the day, he could not find any such person. Finally, he reached a small inn where he decided to spend the night.

The next morning, he woke up to a lot of noise. Walking onto the street, he realized that the ruling king was gathering his troops to invade the neighboring state.

When the king saw the wise man standing at the side of the road, he ordered his army to stop. He got off his horse, walked up to the wise man, and said, 'Oh Great Sage, I am going to war to win the neighboring country so that my country can become even greater. Can you bless me, so I will be victorious?'

After thinking for a moment, the wise man gave the diamond necklace to the king.

The king became annoyed. What good would a diamond necklace be for him. He was already one of the richest kings in the lands. Thus, curiously he asked the Sage, 'Why are you giving me this necklace?'

The Sage explained, 'Oh Great King, I found this valuable necklace yesterday while strolling around the streets of your great city. But I had no use for it. So, I made up my mind to give it to someone in need. I strolled around until the evening in your capital but while looking everywhere, I found no one such a person. Everyone seemed to be living the good life. It seemed that they were all very satisfied with what they had. There was nobody to whom I could give the necklace. But today, it seems that the king of this country still has the desire to gain more possessions. He doesn't seem to be satisfied with what he already has. That's the reason that I felt you were in need of this necklace.'

The King realized his mistake and sent his troops home.

Fortunately, we all hope that wise kings will have wise counsellors and that they also possess a degree of wisdom in selecting them. As this story suggests, the king turned out to be a good listener, but that is rarely the case. In many instances, unfettered greed can have very serious repercussions. As this moral tale suggests, not only can greed be devastating at an individual level, it can also have a very destructive societal impact. In fact, focusing too much on our own immediate possessions may cause us to forget its impact on others and on society as a whole. Looking at the history of humankind, much of the messes that have come about occurred because the leaders who were in charge were not satisfied with what they had. Instead, many of these leaders, past and present, have proven to be deeply wanting. All too often they had forgotten that the purpose of effective leadership is to better the lives of others, instead of taking advantage of their power to satisfy their personal greed. In fact, the victory of greed over love and compassion can always be looked at as the darker side of human nature. As the German philosopher Friedrich Engels said, 'From the first day to this, sheer greed was the driving spirit of civilization.'

Unfortunately, one basic human weakness is our apparent inability to distinguish our needs from our 'greeds'. Thus, if you are susceptible to greed, it would be wise to remind yourself that it will always leave you dissatisfied because you will never be able to get everything you desire. You will never think that you will have enough. As a matter of fact, you can compare greed with a bucket that has a hole in the bottom. You will never be able to fill it up.

Origins

Like envy, some evolutionary psychologists assume that greed is also programmed into our genes. According to them, in the course of our evolution to be greedy was beneficial in promoting our physical survival and reproduction. However, even though there may be some truth in the argument that, given our evolutionary heritage, a degree of greed is inevitable, to be obsessed by greed is another matter altogether. Here I am referring to people who never seem to be content, who are forever dissatisfied, who are continually trying to obtain more things than they need. I am referring to the kinds of people who try to convince themselves that if only they could attain that one desire outside their reach, they would be happy. Of course, what they are aiming for is only a pipe dream. There will always be another desire that follows.

Apart from evolutionary reasons for the presence of greed, another explanation for the phenomenon of greed can be found in early negative developmental experiences. I am thinking of children who were exposed to parental absence, inconsistency or neglect while growing up. Such experiences will leave the developing child with the feeling that something is deeply missing. Consequently, as was the case with envy, greedy people live with the conviction that they are lacking in importance, significance or value, owing to the presence of mental processes that are not necessarily taking place at a conscious level. Fundamentally, they feel unloved. Consequently, they will always be questioning their self-worth. In addition, what may have intensified their greed are experiences of poverty while growing up. In many instances, having listened to the stories told to me by these greedy people, during their childhood, there was very little money to go around. Given their past experiences, they imagine that money will solve all their problems. Money would provide them with feelings of security.[1] Thus, it is possible that three vectors play a role in the greed equation: evolution, parental neglect and poverty.

The results of these various developments are that greedy people appear to have linked their self-worth to their financial worth. Consequently, their main way of keeping score is to go after material things, power and status. In other words, excessive greed is not really a financial issue; it has much more to do with having a troubled mind. Unfortunately, however, in having a troubled mind, greedy people are also causing trouble to others. Overly competitive and aggressive as they are likely to be, they may take ruthless advantage of every opportunity to pursue their wants – and will do so, at any price.

Furthermore, I like to add that an agenda driven by greed is never informed by reflective thought. In fact, greedy individuals, to feel valued, are chasing after illusions. Even though they seem to be pursuing material and other goods, in reality they are looking for something else. They use their materialistic pursuits to find some form of relief for their emotional discomfort. Unfortunately, this search will turn out to be a never-ending pursuit. It will be a mission impossible. Greed easily turns into an addiction. In fact, this kind of behavior is very similar to substance abuse and, as is the case with any

[1] Manfred F. R. Kets de Vries (2021). *The CEO Whisperer: Meditations on Leaders, Life and Change*. London: Palgrave.

addict, their feelings of relief will only last for a short while. Their needs are never satisfied. The release of the neurotransmitter dopamine will only give them a temporary 'high'. As with drugs, there is always going to be the need for another 'fix'. While they are doing what they are doing, what is also quite troublesome is that they have very little understanding of their addictive behavior.

Corruption of the mind

I should add that, like envy, greed will corrupt the mind. Greed can become all consuming, leading to the neglect of the things that are truly important. Naturally, it does not make for wisdom. People in greed's embrace do not realize that what they are really looking for is love, emotional intimacy and unconditional acceptance, including self-acceptance. What they are missing are 'rich', satisfying relationships. Thus, although a modicum of greed may be good for reasons of economic progress, excessive greed is not good for people's well-being. Greed will always exact a very high price.

A famous Zen master took two of his acolytes into a clearing in the forest that was known as a home for wild monkeys. There, he took out a hollow gourd with a small hole in it and inserted sweetened rice, a favorite of monkeys, into the gourd. After having done so, he chained the gourd to a stake and waited in a hideout accompanied by the young monks to see what was going to happen.

Very soon after, a very large monkey approached the gourd, sniffed the rice, inserted his paw, and screeched in frustration when he was unable to withdraw his paw (now balled up as a fist) through the narrow opening. Just then a leopard approached and hearing the monkey screeching decided to have it for dinner.

'Let go of the rice. Run!' screamed the young monks, but to no avail because the monkey, in his desire for the rice, refused to let go. He kept his hand balled up. Consequently, he was caught and eaten by the leopard.

'What killed the monkey?' asked the Zen master. 'The rice,' said one of the young monks. 'Remaining on the ground,' said the other one.

'No,' replied the wise teacher. 'What killed the monkey was nothing but greed.'

When people are caught in the web of greed, their lives will be reduced to little more than a quest to accumulate as much as possible of whatever it is that they covet and crave. Driven by their greed, they may even become reckless and antisocial. In addition, greed has also been associated with negative psychological states such as anxiety, depression and despair, and even with maladaptive behavior patterns such as gambling, hoarding and, not to forget, fraud. Sadly, due to greed, compassion and love will fall by the wayside, contributing to a loosening of family and community ties, thereby undermining the bonds and values upon which society is built.

Wise people realize that greed should be looked at as the ideology of the mediocre. It only makes for psychological rot and from a societal point of view, it has quite dysfunctional effects. Certainly, it does not make for a better world. Thus, our challenge in creating a better world for our children is to transcend the force of greed – to keep these feelings within acceptable boundaries. To be able to do so, however, we will need a certain degree of emotional maturity.

Wise people will be able to transcend the lure of greed, given the lessons of life they have acquired over time. Hopefully, they will also be able to transfer their concerns about this tempting vice to the next generation. I am referring to the ability to care for others. In fact, there is a lot of wisdom in enjoying seeing other people grow, teaching them lessons of life and experiencing this sense of generativity.[2] People who are wise take exception to Groucho Marx's rather flippant statement: 'Why should I care about future generations – what have they ever done for me?' Like the way the Zen master was teaching the young monks, they seek to create an increased awareness of greed's darker side.

This brings me to the question of whether greed is something that affects your life. Is it influencing the way you live? Does it affect your leadership style? If so, what are you doing to prevent the siren's song of greed from gaining the upper hand?

Remember, if morality comes up against greed, all too often morality will lose out. Therefore, if you want to pursue wisdom, it would be good to keep in mind the comment of Seneca, 'It is not the man who has little, but he who desires more, that is poor.' To illustrate this point, this very old classic fairy tale may be another warning, once more demonstrating that insatiable greed devours common sense:

---

[2] Erik H. Erikson (1950). *Childhood and Society*. New York: W. W. Norton.

Once upon a time, in land far away, there lived a farmer with his family. They lived in great poverty. To survive, the farmer and his wife grew some vegetables, some of which he sold at the market-place. As time went by, they saved up enough money to buy a goose. The goose, however, turned out to be a magic goose as it laid one golden egg each day. Every day, the farmer sold this golden egg to buy things for his family. Slowly but steadily, the family became richer and richer.

But it was not long before the farmer grew impatient with the goose because she gave him only one single egg a day. He felt that he was not getting rich fast enough. Thus, a very wicked idea came to the farmer's mind. 'If the magic goose lays one golden egg every day, how many golden eggs will be inside the goose? If I cut open the goose, I could be richer much faster.'

With this thought in mind, the farmer killed the goose and opened her belly. But when the deed was done, not a single golden egg was to be found. Because of his greed, the farmer had lost his goose and the golden eggs.

Listening

A closed mouth catches no flies.

—Miguel de Cervantes

There's a lot of difference between hearing and listening.

—Gilbert Chesterton

Lesson 5: Listening

Listening and speaking are the basic communication tools that we use every day. Naturally, the best way to understand people is to listen to them, but all too often, we take listening merely for granted. If we do not know how to listen effectively, however, it will be a real challenge to understand what other people are trying to say. Truth be told, by and large, most people prefer to talk, but they do not realize that too much talking will be a barrier to effective communication. They do not heed the words spoken in the *Book of Proverbs*: 'Even a fool, who keeps quiet, is considered wise, discerning, if he seals his lips.' The Zen Masters also put it quite succinctly: 'The one who knows, does not say. The one who says, does not know.' They know that wise people know how to listen.

Listening implies inviting another person into your life. Listening is about making space for the other person, but as you may have discovered for yourself, to create this space is not always easy. In many instances, if you would be prepared to do a time and motion study, you may discover that while you think that you are engaged in an interchange of give-and-take, in reality, you are spending most of your life speaking. In fact, most of us spend only a very small portion of the time listening to what is being said. The truth of the matter is that we like to talk. The trouble is that, all too often, we like to show off how much we know. By acting in such a way, this suggests that we are not really interested in learning new things. What may be more important is the game of one-upmanship. For many people, listening seems to be nothing more than a period during which they are working out what they plan to say next. Of course, by behaving in this manner, there will be very little wisdom in the interchange.

Unfortunately, as you may also have discovered if you have been at the receiving end of such a dialogue or better said, monologue, many highly intelligent and knowledgeable people are not always the best of listeners. Many of them, do not listen with the intent to understand. In fact, as I am suggesting, they only seem to listen with the intent to reply. They are too preoccupied in coming up with clever responses. Of course, by behaving in this manner, there is going to be very little wisdom in the interchange. Let us consider the story of the four monks.

Four monks decided to meditate silently without speaking for two weeks. They lit a candle as a symbol of their practice and began. By nightfall on the first day, the candle flickered and then went out.

The first monk said: 'Oh, no! The candle is out.'

The second monk said: 'We're not supposed to talk!'

The third monk said: 'Why must you two break the silence?'

The fourth monk laughed and said: 'Ha! I'm the only one who didn't speak.'

It did not look like there was a fifth monk present who was able to keep his mouth shut. None of the monks seemed to be familiar with the famous Japanese Zen kōan of the sound of one hand clapping. Most probably, what this Zen story is trying to convey is the importance of silence, listening and contemplation. Listening is the way to learn – to receive new knowledge – or as the Dalai Lama said, 'When you talk, you are only repeating what you already know. But if you listen, you may learn something new.' Is the reason why we have two ears and only one mouth that we should listen more and talk less? Thus, it should not come as a surprise that wise people tend to listen more. No wonder that the statues of the Buddha show him to have ears that are proportionately very large compared to his body.

Although you may be subliminally aware that what I am saying is true, to listen or not to listen will always be a challenging proposition. Therefore, it does not hurt to constantly remind yourself that listening is the way to obtain a deeper understanding of what the other person is trying to convey. In fact, if you make a real effort to listen, you may understand why the other person wants to talk to you in the first place.

Pseudo-listening

The reason listening can be so difficult appears to be our narcissistic disposition. Too often, we pretend to be listening while our mind is racing in trying to think of something clever. However, as I have said before, being clever is not being wise. In addition, to exacerbate our narcissistic tendencies, there is also the kind of listening with half an ear that presumes that we already know what the other person is going to say. I am referring to an inattentive listening, only waiting for a chance to speak, and even becoming impatient, wishing to get rid of the other person. As the philosopher and poet Ralph Waldo Emerson once said, 'There is a difference between truly listening and waiting for your turn to talk.' This urge to interrupt and get a word in can be quite powerful. Some people just want to hear themselves speak just to confirm and validate their existence. It has been said that big egos have little ears.

Furthermore, you had better realize that you cannot truly listen to anyone and do something else at the same time. Multi-tasking will never be a good idea. Even though you may not think so, multi-tasking does not work well. Actually, as some studies have shown, switching from one task to the next can reduce your productivity by as much as forty per cent.[1] This kind of selective listening can also be quite irritating to the person on the other end. It is not very respectful.

Thus, the question that always should be at the top of your mind is: are you listening or is your mind somewhere

---

[1]Joshua S. Rubinstein, David E. Meyer and Jeffrey E. Evans (2001). Executive control of cognitive processes in task switching. *Journal of Experimental Psychology: Human Perception and Performance*, 27 (4), 763–797.

else? Are you so self-centered that it is difficult to pay attention to the other person? If you have the wish to be a good listener, however, it is important to never allow your ego to diminish your ability to listen. In fact, you need to liberate yourself from the prison of your ego-centric world, but, given the narcissistic disposition of *Homo sapiens*, this attempt to become a compassionate, listening human being is not easy. It could be a lifelong learning project.

Being a good talker

It is important to note that there is no direct relationship between wisdom and eloquence. As the Swiss philosopher Jean Jacques Rousseau noted, 'People who know little are usually great talkers, while men who know much say little.' Many people who come across as great talkers often demonstrate very few signs of wisdom. As a matter of fact, many things that they are saying may not even make much sense. Some of these people seem to be suffering from some kind of verbal diarrhea. It appears as though they are unable to synchronize their associative thoughts with the words spoken. The way they articulate their ideas becomes too free flowing, thus not providing sufficient closure. The proverb, 'Everybody is wise until they speak,' very much applies to these people. As the mathematician Ivan Panin once wrote, 'The wise man hath his thoughts in his head; the fool, on his tongue.' In contrast, it is often silence that is the sound that nourishes wisdom. In fact, there can be real wisdom in keeping your mouth shut. You may even have discovered for yourself that the quieter you are, the more you will hear. Furthermore, you may also have discovered that the less you talk, the more you will be listened to.

Wise people know when and when not to speak. They have come to realize that whenever words are spoken, if inappropriate, they may have to eat those words afterwards. In other words, they have learned that there can be enormous power in silence. They know that the gift of good listening is that it makes people want to speak with them. Nasrudin seemed to be well aware of it.

> *A man approached Nasrudin and asked him, 'How does one become wise?' To which Nasrudin replied: 'Listen attentively to wise people when they speak. And when someone is listening to you, listen attentively to what you are saying!'*

Using yourself as an instrument

You can learn so much from listening; you can learn so much from really listening; and you can learn so much from really listening not only to others, but also to yourself. Concerning the latter, while listening, I am referring to the importance of paying attention to your inner dialogue, to the thoughts and feelings that the other party arouses in you. What takes place in this bi-personal field is described by psychoanalysts as transference and counter-transference reactions.[2] Thus, what the other party is doing to you very much warrants attention. It will always be an additional source of information.

---

[2] Charles J. Gelso and Jeffrey Hayes (2007). *Countertransference and the Therapist's Inner Experience: Perils and Possibilities*. Mahwah, NJ: Lawrence Erlbaum; Manfred F. R. Kets de Vries (2021). *The CEO Whisperer: Meditations on Leadership, Life and Change*. London: Palgrave.

Wise listeners listen with their eyes as well as their ears. As a matter of fact, they listen with all their senses. They use themselves, as I have said often, 'as an instrument'. To be able to really understand what the other has to say, they try to be quiet enough to really hear what is going on in their own head. It is the information that the other evokes in them that will provide them with greater insights. To be able to engage in all of these activities simultaneously will not be an easy task, however. To single out the main themes presented by the other person, and to listen to your inner dialogue, can be like solving riddles. If you are able to do so, however, both parties will experience an ever-widening expression of growth and development.

What's not being said

Sometimes it is not what a person says, but rather what the other does not say that will tell you more than their words ever could. Therefore, as a listener, you should not only pay attention to the emerging verbal but also the non-verbal clues. You should make a conscious effort to not only hear the words, but also to listen to the speaker's intent. Thus, deep listeners always pay attention to the music that plays underneath the words that are spoken and not spoken.

Furthermore, it is vital that if *you* decide to talk, that you appreciate how the other person is listening, how he or she will interpret, process and assign meaning to what you are saying to him or her. However, if you are able to effectively engage in this delicate discourse of give-and-take, it will be a great way to influence the other person. It will enrich the conversation and it will turn the conversation into a true dialogue. Both parties may be really listening to what is communicated.

If you are able to pick up these conscious and unconscious communications, the conversation will enter into a much deeper level, and so will your relationship. As a matter of fact, you may even become a role model for effective and positive communication. What is more, as a skilled listener, you can help other people tap into their own wisdom.

Whose agenda?

As I have emphasized before, deep listening requires an intentional effort to focus on the other person, to pay attention to his or her agenda. Moreover, it requires compassion; it requires empathy. We listen to truly understand the other person. Always remind yourself that deep listening is a strongly vicarious experience. It is a moment of deep engagement, whereby you have to make an effort to let go of your own needs.

Thus, we listen because we want to understand. We listen because we care. It is the reason that wise listeners know how to put their ego aside. Feeling secure within themselves, they are also not worried to be swept away by the other person's emotions. Also, wise listeners do not have this compelling need to make their presence known. They are open to receive, to welcome, to accept. As I have suggested before, they make their comments sparingly. They tend to ask insightful questions to further the conversation. Staying quiet, however, does not mean that they have nothing to say. They are merely more careful about the use of words. Wise people seem to be more fluent in silence. Also, they know how to filter important from irrelevant information.

If you have attained a modicum of wisdom, you may have also understood that just because you want to say certain things, does not mean that you need to say it. You need to judge what is the appropriate time. Furthermore, you may decide – whatever you would like to say – that the other person is not yet ready to hear it. As I say quite often, 'Only strike when the iron is cold.' Again, there will be times when silence is the best answer. It may explain why, as I have said before, the wiser you are, the more you are inclined to keep your mouth shut. In addition, at times, it will also be quite wise to overlook things. After all, wise people know, once they have said what they may wish to say, that their words can only be forgiven, not forgotten. A short tale that is credited to Socrates may be of use here.

One day, in ancient Greece, an acquaintance encountered Socrates, the great philosopher and said, 'Do you know what I just heard about your friend?'

'Hold on a minute,' Socrates replied. 'Before telling me anything I'd like you to pass a little test. It's called the Triple Filter Test.'

'What do you mean by triple filter?'

'Let me tell you,' Socrates continued. 'Before you talk to me about my friend, it might be a good idea to take a moment and filter what you're going to say. That's why I call it the triple filter test. The first filter is Truth. Have you made absolutely sure that what you are about to tell me is true?'

'No,' the acquaintance said, 'Actually I just heard about it and ....'

'All right,' said Socrates. 'So, you don't really know if it's true or not. Now let's try the second filter, the filter of Goodness. Is what you are about to tell me about my friend something good?'

'No, on the contrary.'

'So,' Socrates continued, 'you want to tell me something bad about him, but you're not certain it's true. You may still pass the test though, because there's one filter left: the filter of Usefulness. Is what you want to tell me about my friend going to be useful to me?'

'I don't think so.'

'Well,' concluded Socrates, 'if what you want to tell me is neither true nor good nor even useful, why bother to tell it to me at all?'

The art of deep listening

As must have become clear by now, deep listening is the art and practice of putting someone else's speaking, thinking and feeling needs ahead of your own. If you possess this very gift, people do want to speak with you. This gift means that you really listen and do not barge in with your own thoughts. Instead, you are showing real interest in what the other person has to say. You also may have come to realize that when someone is in psychological distress and feels really listened to – without being judged – that it can have a very positive therapeutic effect. There is something to be said for cathartic experiences. Opening up can be quite liberating. It takes the other person beyond just intellectually assessing adverse situations. It may further the understanding of what is being felt.

In other words, the experience of being heard – by putting yourself in the other person's shoes – can be extremely restorative. As I have mentioned earlier, showing compassion and empathy can have great healing powers. After all, all of us would like to have an empathetic ear to be listened to. Furthermore, it is important to realize that the experience of being listened to means a lot more than just having your ideas heard. It can also be seen as a sign of respect. If you are the one who wants to tell your story – and someone is prepared to listen – it will make you feel valued. In addition, the possibility of telling your story to a good listener also fosters emotional and intellectual reflection. It may provide you with a deeper insight of why certain things are troublesome to you. You may gain an understanding of how it is related to other incidents in your life. The unexpected action of being really listened to can even create a space of transformation capable of shattering complacency and despair.

If you are the listener, always remember what is important is to understand what matters to the other person, not only what is important to you. You never really understand a person until you consider things from his or her point of view. As I explained in Chapter 2, empathy is a cognitive and emotive process – to inhabit another person's view of the world is to feel the world with the other. However, to be able to do so, you must always try to put yourself in the place of the person who is speaking. It comes down to an effort to experience the emotions of other people, to understand what they are trying to say and why. Thus, if you possess this gift of deep listening – if you take the time to understand and show that you really care – you will contribute to the other's sense of dignity and self-worth.

While you are deep listening, it is also essential – difficult as it can be – to remain non-judgemental. You need to be able to suspend your sense of disbelief; you need to suspend your own feelings and thoughts. If you behave in this manner, however, you will create a feeling of safety that will contribute to feelings of trust and, with trust, it will be more likely that the speaker will open up. He or she will be more willing to be vulnerable. In fact, the art of active listening is how to make the other person feel valued, respected and safe.

The listening leader

The writer Mark Twain once said, 'Wisdom is the reward you get for a lifetime of listening when you would have rather talked.' As must have become clear by now, the wiser you are, the less you talk. In a world where there is too much noise and not enough reflection, deep listening to what people have to say will be critical. In particular, this quality will be an important one for the leaders of our present-day world. Unfortunately, it is for all to see that listening leaders are quite rare. Given the kind of character types that rise to leadership positions, listening does not seem to be one of their major qualities. Most of them are too preoccupied with their own needs. Instead of listening, they prefer to make a lot of noise. Clearly, they prefer to talk. In addition, it looks like many of them are running somewhat convoluted reality shows that cater to people's wish to believe. Magical thinking is more their specialty. As William Shakespeare said quite astutely, 'The empty vessel makes the loudest sound.' Many leaders talk much but do not know how to listen; they tend to be more in a telling than a listening mode. As a result, they do not pick up the subtle signals of what their constituency is trying to tell them.

However, it is listening leaders that the world needs most. Such leaders do not force their commands on people. Instead, they pay attention to the concerns of their people. By truly listening, they create a deep understanding of what needs to be done to support their constituencies and truly listening helps them set the pace for the change that a society needs. They are not salesmen of illusions. They are reality driven.

From a more personal perspective, looking at your own life, it is clear how valuable real listening can be. In looking back at your personal history, you should ask yourself the question, how many mistakes have you made because you did not listen well? How could these mistakes have been prevented? Thus, given your experience, you would be wise to keep in mind that wisdom is the reward that you get for a lifetime of listening when you would have rather preferred to talk. Practice listening and start to really listen right now, in whatever context!

9

Choose your battles wisely

If you know the enemy and know yourself, you need not fear the result of a hundred battles. If you know yourself, but not the enemy, for every victory gained you will also suffer a defeat. If you know neither the enemy nor yourself, you will succumb in every battle.

—Sun Tzu

He who fights with monsters might take care lest he thereby become a monster. And if you gaze for long into an abyss, the abyss gazes also into you.

—Friedrich Nietzsche

Lesson 6: Choose your battles wisely

Once upon a time, in Spain, there lived a gentleman whose name was Don Quixote. All day and night he dreamed of doing glorious deeds, going into battle and saving damsels in distress. Eventually, assisted by his faithful servant Sancho Panza, he decided to go on an adventure to fight his battles.

As they went their way, on a wide, open plain, they came upon the sight of a number of windmills. Don Quixote cried out: 'Fortune guides our path, Sancho! Look at all these giants ahead! I will fight them and defeat them. It will bring us rich rewards.'

But Sancho Panza only said quite clear-headedly, 'Where are these giants? I don't see any giants.'

'Don't you see?' Don Quixote said. 'They're just ahead of you. Surely you see their long arms threatening us.'

'But sir,' Sancho Panza responded, 'these aren't giants. These are just windmills.'

Don Quixote shook his head and responded sadly, 'Clearly, my friend, you aren't a real adventurer. Can't you see these are giants? But I understand. If you're afraid, I will battle them alone.'

With that Don Quixote spurred on his horse and galloped towards the windmills, ready to engage in battle.

Galloping along, he shouted, 'Don't run away, you cowards! I'm ready to do battle.' After having said these words, Don Quixote charged one of the windmills.

Exactly at that moment, the wind started to blow and the arms of the windmill began to spin.

'Oh, monster! How dare you to threaten me,' Don Quixote shouted.

He galloped up to the windmill and thrust his lance through one of the arms, but the lance broke. The arm of the windmill lifted Quixote up into the air, making him go around and around, until he tumbled down and fell upon the grass.

A sign of wisdom is to choose your battles wisely. Unfortunately, too many people seem to be fighting windmills. In fact, Don Quixote's fight with the windmills is another reminder that wise counsel can be important. Each of us would be wise to check the facts before entering battle. I should add that it does not hurt to listen to good advice. Don Quixote, however, ignored the advice of his servant

Sancho Panza. He took the windmills for giants and charged blindly ahead. Needless to say, the windmills did not do badly in the joust.

The moral of the story in Miguel de Cervantes' novel is that the judgements you make can be quite quixotic. Like Don Quixote, you may prefer to ignore wise council and just charge ahead. You may dismiss any form of reflection, become blinded and ignore reality. Therefore, when all is said and done, before you enter the battlefield, you would be wise to reflect on what motivates you to do so in the first place. In fact, if you would take a moment's pause, you might change your mind.

The expression to choose your battles wisely is attributed to the Chinese military strategist, Sun Tzu, a renowned general of the ancient Chinese army. The main idea of his admonishment is to think wisely – to look at the larger picture – before you engage in battle. Truth be told, it is an important admonition. As a matter of fact, you are facing many battles each day, knowingly or unknowingly. Given these encounters, you would do well to be prepared. For example, you may have arguments with family members, friends, colleagues at work, with people while taking the underground or have a misunderstanding with a shop keeper – the list goes on. Many times, each day, you have to choose which battles are worth fighting. If you 'fight' too many, however, it can become overwhelming, cumbersome and very exhausting. That is the reason why knowing which battles to pick becomes so important.

Naturally, before choosing 'to battle', you should ask yourself if there needs to be a battle in the first place, but if you think that you have no choice but to battle, you had better ask yourself whether it is your battle or the battle of somebody else. To fight a battle that actually belongs to someone else is an easy mistake to make. To get locked into unnecessary conflicts can easily occur. Furthermore, you would be wise to remind yourself that if you do not choose your battles wisely, you may end up being too tired to fight the truly important ones.

You may have been in situations where you found yourself fighting a battle that you never really wanted to be part of. You may have become involved in an argument about something that really was not important enough to fight for. Thus, what I am trying to say is that there is great value in being selective about whether you want to fight at all. Wise generals know that it is not wise to fight many battles all at once, and on too many fronts. If so, you would become too vulnerable and, what is more (as I mentioned previously), you will be too tired to fight the really important battles. The obvious conclusion is, if you want to avoid undue stress, that you must make a point of not getting upset about everything. To make mountains out of molehills is never a good idea.

'Pre-battle' questions

What I am emphasizing is that wise people know how to separate the important from the less important matters. They are quite selective in dealing with problems, arguments and confrontations, and they are very cognizant of the fact that every battle they get into will consume much time and energy. In addition, they realize that some things simply will not matter in the long run. What 'battles' are really worth fighting? Let us turn to another story, this time about a general of antiquity.

It was going to be an important battle. The general decided to launch an attack though his army was greatly outnumbered. Although he was confident of victory, his men were filled with great apprehension. He knew that he had a morale problem. On the way to the battlefield, the general decided to stop at a small shrine known for its miracles. After everyone offered prayers, the general took a coin from his pocket and said to his soldiers, 'I'm going to toss this coin to see what destiny will have in store for us. I wonder what the shrine is going to tell us. I had a dream last night that revealed if it is heads, we will be victorious, but if it is tails, we will lose.'

The soldiers watched intently. The coin spun through the air, glinting and landed – it was heads! Overjoyed, highly motivated, the army marched to battle and vanquished the enemy.

Later, a lieutenant was pondering over the day's events with the general. 'Luckily, no one can alter destiny, sir,' he said.

'How true,' replied the general and showed his fellow soldier the coin. Both sides had heads!

I guess that the general had the wisdom to know something about motivation. He knew what to do about the morale of his soldiers. In addition, he must have believed that the battle was important enough to engage. Clearly, he kept the bigger picture in mind and he must have thought that, with the right motivation, he had a good chance to be victorious. Often, however, looking at other 'battles', that is not the case.

In fact, do you think that a life is well lived if you worried about every little thing? Should you be arguing with everyone who is standing in your way? To be perfectly honest, you know that is not a very wise thing to do. It is not the way to live life. You know that a well-lived life means spending your time on the things that really matter. Like the general in the story, you should know when to battle and when to let it be. In fact, you may have figured out by now that an important aspect of life's happiness consists not in fighting battles, but in avoiding them.

Ultimately, the point of choosing your battles wisely is to be strategic in how you spend that limited resource called time and energy. Thus, if you decide 'to battle', you should consider not only what's going to happen immediately, but also how this battle will work out in the longer run. You should ask yourself whether you really want to be battling the small things of life. Do you really want to fight about things that have little meaning later on? Thus, if you are wise, you pay attention to its future consequences and to the things that really matter. In addition, people who possess wisdom also take into consideration how a battle will affect the people who are important to them. By making the choice as to what battles they want to fight, they will be 'winning' the big game that is called life.

I fight, thus I'm alive

Of course, there will always be people who seem to enjoy arguments for arguments' sake. Fighting seems to be their preferred way of life. They always are trying to get a rise out of others. It is as if they are inspired by the motto, 'I fight, thus I'm alive'. As a matter of fact, some of these people seem to be perpetually angry and, given their personal history, they may have their reasons. They may also be the kind of people who always want to be right. I am referring to people who are not exactly open-minded. On the contrary, often it is their way or the highway. What these people do not realize, however, is that 'rightism' does not make for a peaceful life. In fact, it will make for a very troubled existence. Some of these people never seem to be able to recognize what kinds of battles would be really important to them.

Therefore, when you come in proximity to such people, if at all possible, the wisest thing to do is to stay away from them. Given their personality makeup, they will only be inviting trouble. If not, you may just get pulled down into their negative pit of misery. After all, the road to hell is paved with the bones of people who do not know when to quit fighting. It is useful to always keep this saying in mind: 'Never wrestle with a pig. You both get dirty, and the pig likes it.' In other words, you better make wise choices!

Making choices

One evening as a famous Zen master was meditating, a thief with a sharp sword entered his hut, demanding either money or his life.

The Zen master told him: 'Please, don't disturb me now. If you need money, just look in that drawer.' After saying so, he resumed his meditation.

A short time later, he stopped his meditation and called: 'Please, don't take all the money. I need some of it to pay a small debt tomorrow.'

The burglar left some money behind and started to leave.

When he was almost out of the door, the Zen master said: 'You should thank a person when you receive a gift.' The thief thanked him and took off.

A few days later, the thief was caught and confessed the various things he had done, including stealing the money from the Zen master.

When the Zen master was called as a witness, he said: 'This man is no thief, at least as far as I am concerned. I gave him money and he thanked me for it.'

After he had finished his prison term, the man went to the Zen master and became his disciple.

Life is not about being constantly on the battlefield. At times, as seen in this story, it is wiser to play emotional judo. The Zen master made some kind of paradoxical intervention.[1] In a way, he instructed the thief to perform the very act he should stop doing. Instead of having a fight, he ended up having a disciple. Therefore, if you do not want to be burned out before entering the battlefield, you had better do some kind of cost-benefit analysis. You should reflect on what criteria you want to use for passing up one battle and choosing to engage in another. When faced with a challenging situation, you could ask yourself the following questions:

- Keep on reminding yourself to only fight for things that are truly important. Ask yourself whether entering a particular 'battle' will be worth your time and energy.

[1] Gerald R. Weeks, and Luciano L'Abayte (1982). *Paradoxical Psychotherapy: Theory and Practice*. New York: Brunner/Mazel.

Also, make an effort to consider the possible outcomes of such a battle. What do you see as the downside risks? Thus, before you fight, evaluate its consequences. In other words, always let go of the trivial but fight for the vital. Also, ask yourself, how will whatever you plan to do affect the limited resources that you have available? (These resources include your time, your emotional capital, the goodwill of others, your reputation and possibly even include financial costs.) On the benefit side, try to assess how likely it is that you will 'win' and what a difference it will make for you and others if you win. You may even conclude that many of the things you are concerned about presently may not really be important in the long run. Thus, always ask yourself how this battle will impinge on the bigger picture that is your life. In fact, if you go through this exercise, you may come to realize that a masterly retreat – to succeed without fighting – may be in itself the greatest victory.

- Furthermore, you should also ask yourself whether the issue is really a problem or is there something else – much deeper – that is troubling you. If so, what are the underlying reasons for your irritation? Try to understand what is happening beneath the surface. In addition, you would also be wise to remind yourself that if you choose to fight every battle that comes your way, you will create a bad reputation for yourself.
- When you are in a fighting mood, however, take a moment to calm down and think the matter through. Try to avoid reacting immediately. Once again, take some time to review your motivation of why you want to enter this battle. Will it only give you a short-term or

transitory benefit? Is there a low probability of winning without doing excessive damage? Is it an issue where you will have a small win, but lose in terms of relationships? Another important question to ask yourself is, if you do not fight this battle (regardless of whether you win it or lose it), will you be able to live with yourself afterwards? At a later date, would you be able to face yourself in the mirror to say to yourself that you made a decision that you really believed was right at the time? Going through this kind of reflective activity, you may come to realize that winning may not be as important as it originally appeared to be.

- If you decide to go into battle, however, try to communicate why you are doing so. If possible, have a respectful conversation with the other party and during these conversations, practice active, deep listening. Let the other person know that his or her view is valued, even if you disagree. If the situation becomes too tense, it may be wise to take a break. It is better to take a step away than letting the argument escalate. In addition, while in the midst of a battle, do not assume that the other party knows what you are feeling. In fact, in trying to look at the situation through the eyes of your opponent, you may be able to completely change the dynamics of the argument. You may come to realize that both parties have contributed to the problem. By taking this perspective, the understanding you acquire may help you to meet each other halfway. You may find a way to compromise. Always remember, it is better to work towards a win-win solution whereby both parties appear to emerge victorious. In fact, there is nothing victorious about bringing your 'opponent' down. However, when you cannot reach an agreement, while wanting to keep your relationship intact, it may be time to look for professional advice. Some issues are too formidable to solve only by yourself. Sometimes a coach, psychotherapist, counsellor or mediator can bring clarity to a situation that is stuck.

- Of course, whenever possible, do your best to prevent the emergence of the problem. A little prevention can go a very long way. Try to address the situation as soon as you see an issue that may come up. Be proactive in your approach. Some arguments are simply a difference in perspective.

If you know your 'enemy' and know yourself, you will be more equipped to fight battles without it having a disastrous effect. Actually, in many instances, it is much better to conquer yourself than to go on to the battlefield. History is full of tragic examples of battles that could have been prevented if the parties had skillfully used their negotiation skills instead of entering a war. The capacity to negotiate and the ability to resolve differences are true signs of human wisdom.

Mahatma Gandhi once said, 'Nobody can hurt me without my permission.' Leaders of organizations, communities and countries should keep this in mind. All too often, they choose to go into battle. To arrive at some form of damage control, however, they would do well to look at the battles that are taking place within. Often, what count are the struggles within yourself – the scenes that unfold in your inner theatre. If you understand what is really important to you, you may be more selective about your battles. You will be more prepared to decide what can be a good or a bad battle. Knowing where that line sits will help you to direct your efforts better, an observation that is especially valid in leadership situations.

In that respect, in the context of the future battles in your life, you would be wise to go through the following thought experiment: Imagine you are lying on your deathbed. While your life is passing by, what would you like to see? What has been really important? How would you like to be remembered? Keeping what is important in mind, what will be the battles worth fighting and how will these reflections make you a more effective leader?

10

Courage

Courage is the first of human qualities because it is the quality which guarantees the others.

—Aristotle

Grant me the serenity to accept the things I cannot change, courage to change the things I can . . . give us courage to change what must be altered, serenity to accept what cannot be helped, and the insight to know the one from the other.

—Reinhold Niebuhr

Lesson 7: Courage

Human history is full of tales whereby people showed courage. To take a well-known example, there is the Ballad of Mulan, a poem that tells the tale of a courageous female warrior known as Mulan, who supposedly lived in China during the Northern and Southern dynasties period (between 420 and 589 CE). It is an intriguing story, even though it is widely believed that the story about her life is a fictional one. However, real or not real, the tale describes a woman who decides to go against tradition by becoming a warrior.

In the original poem, Hua Mulan is sitting at her loom as the men in her family are asked to join the army to defend China. As she does not want her old and sickly father to serve in the army and as her brother is far too young, she decides to take her father's place with the blessing of both parents. As Mulan was already a good fighter who had been trained in martial arts, sword fighting and archery, she proves her worth by overcoming many challenges. In the process she not only is bringing honor to her family by helping to save the Chinese empire but is also demonstrating that a woman can do things as well as a man.

After years of military campaign and service to her country, Mulan returns to her hometown with honor and gifts from the emperor. Her parents, sister and younger brother hurry to welcome her and prepare a feast to celebrate her return. Mulan changes her clothes, makes up her hair and face and greets her fellow soldiers, who, when they see her transformed as a woman, are shocked. Fighting side-by-side with her for years, they were not aware that Mulan was not a man.

Some adaptations of this story have cast Mulan as a national heroine. Often, she is presented as an iconic symbol to boost people's spirit, given her courage to fight against invaders into China, but the underlining message of her story is worth noting. Mulan's transgression (in pretending to be a man) has been honorable (she did it to save her father and serve her country). In addition, it was an activity that turned out to be successful. Furthermore, whatever masculine activities she undertook, they were mitigated in the end as she returned home to resume her life as a woman. Thus, not only has Mulan been exemplary in showing courage, but, at the same time, she is non-threatening to the social structure, at least to the social structure of that period. Perhaps, that is what has given the Mulan story such an enduring, universal appeal. It turned into a journey of discovery and self-exploration and, naturally, in being able to play the role of the courageous warrior, it showed us another facet of the female persona.

Not only did Mulan show *physical* courage – given her feats on the battlefield – she also showed great *moral* courage in doing what she thought was right. Here, I am referring to her steadfastness in the face of likely disapproval by impersonating a male warrior. She knew that many people would find fault with her if they knew that she was a woman. However, she had assumed the role of warrior for a higher purpose; she was trying to serve the common good.

'Courage is wisdom,' according to Socrates. The philosopher Baltasar Gracián shared that core principle when he noted, 'without courage, wisdom bears no fruit', something realized by Mulan. Wisdom and courage – probably the most valued of the virtues – have always been in high demand and the choices we make in life are very much influenced by them. Guided by these virtues, ordinary people are able to do extraordinary things, and as could be seen, Mulan took heart. In fact, courage is really a 'heart word'. The root of the word courage is *cor* – the Latin word for heart. In one of its earliest forms, the word 'courage' meant 'to speak one's mind by telling all one's heart'.

Sometimes, wisdom is labelled as being the predecessor of courage, and perhaps, with wisdom, courage will be inevitable. Conversely, at times, courage has been portrayed as being a precursor of wisdom, the logic being that you need to be able to take courageous action if you are pursuing wisdom. It is the kind of challenging education that is required if you desire to be wise.

In fact, courage has many different dimensions. You can look at courage as a core human quality pertaining to such strengths as valor (taking a physical, intellectual and emotional stance in the face of danger); authenticity (representing yourself to others and to yourself in a sincere fashion); enthusiasm (as in passionately approaching challenging situations); and perseverance (hanging in there/being able to pursue challenging tasks to completion). In other words, with courage, action needs to follow. Thus, to show courage does not just mean dreaming about something. On the contrary, it also means doing something.

When you are courageous, whatever action you take will be difficult. To act courageously often implies that you will be uncomfortable since you have to take risks, face uncertainty and may fail. In other words, to act courageously means getting out of your comfort zone. It implies standing up for what you believe in, even when others do not feel the same way. In addition, courage may refer to selfless behavior. Often, with courage, you will be displaying concern for others rather than just for yourself. Of course, having said all of this, there is always going to be a fine line between courage and stupidity. In other words, you should not confuse courage with foolhardiness. Wise people, however, recognize when courage ends and when stupidity begins.

To think for yourself

Courage is also associated with self-confidence. It takes courage to be yourself. It takes courage to think for yourself. And it takes courage to believe in yourself. To behave in an authentic way can be difficult, but courageous people don't let the noise of other people's opinions drown out their inner voice. They realize that they have to take responsibility for their own life. Courageous people will have the courage to be who they are, not what other people expect them to be. Although they may not necessarily realize it consciously, without courage, their real self will never emerge. If so, they will always have to deal with a somewhat divided self, having to struggle with feeling inauthentic. In that respect, courage is associated with making the best out of your life, to never limit the expectations you have of yourself and to never settle for anything less than what you are truly capable of achieving.

Naturally, it will take a lot of courage to let go of the familiar and the seemingly secure. It will take courage to embrace the new and to put yourself in uncomfortable situations. Courageous people have concluded, however, that there is no true security in what is no longer meaningful. They prefer doing what they think is right, no matter what other people have to say about it. They strongly believe that keeping their heads low will not help them move forward. In fact, courage can be looked at as the magic key to living life with integrity and authenticity. After all, as I am suggesting, a life lived without courage is a life half lived, and surely it does not make for living wisely.

In fact, many people seem to have two lives: the life they live and the unlived life within them. It is what makes for a somewhat divided self, the kind of experience that I referred to in Chapter 3. If that is the case, these people experience the need to wear a mask, a persona, to present themselves in a more sociably desirable way, but, in doing so, there is always the danger that they might lose their own individuality to this persona. They may end up turning into a rather shallow, unstable, conformist kind of personality, overly concerned about what other people think. The pressure to always put on a mask – to always conform – is not a good prescription for courage.

Courage is risking the known for the unknown, to release the familiar and seemingly secure. It also implies showing grace under pressure. Conversely, in staying only with the known, you may be living a life half lived. Whatever you do, however, showing courage will always be a love affair with the unknown, or, to quote the American writer William Faulkner, 'You cannot swim for new horizons until you have courage to lose sight of the shore.' In other words, you cannot find anything new if you are unwilling to leave the shore. Unfortunately, people who lack courage will always find ways to justify their actions. When you keep your head down when things are wrong, rationalizing it as a wise course of action, you are in reality confusing wisdom with cowardice. When you choose to stand back up, you are using wisdom to overcome cowardice.

Being fearful

When Nikita Khrushchev pronounced his famous denunciation of Stalin, someone in the Congress Hall is reported to have said, 'Where were you, Comrade Khrushchev, when all those innocent people were being slaughtered?'

Khrushchev paused, looked round the Hall, and said, 'Will the person who said that kindly stand up!'

Tension mounted in the Hall. No one moved.

Said Khrushchev, 'Well, whoever you are, you have your answer now. I was in exactly the same position then as you find yourself in now.'

Nelson Mandela noted, 'I learned that courage was not the absence of fear, but the triumph over it.' Courage is walking toward what you would rather run away from, to persevere in the face of fear. For example, if you decide to go parachute jumping and you, to some extent, are not fearful, you are either crazy or unaware. Thus, courage is being able to face fear in a realistic way, defining it, considering alternatives and deciding to go ahead in spite of the calculated risks.

In fact, you should keep in mind in the context of courage, that its opposite is not necessarily cowardice. The more appropriate name would be conformity – being unwilling to deal with uncomfortable situations. However, should your fears of creating trouble not give way to the only real danger, which is that of never trying? Thus, courage is not just overcoming fear, but rather taking a stand in spite of all your fears. It is the ability to contain your fears, to be able to progress with whatever you have set out to do in your life. As can be seen over and over again, many people have failed in life because they did nothing about their fears, fearful as they were of displaying courage.

Doing what is right

What should be kept in mind is that whatever course of action you decide to take, there is always someone to tell you that you are wrong, and given your inner doubts, you might think that these critics are right. However, what makes you stand out – what makes you act courageously – is to do what you think is the right thing even when nobody else is doing so. It implies standing up for what you believe in, even if you have to stand alone. Courage means standing up for truth, regardless of who steps on it. Again, I would like to reiterate that living a full life is not about choosing the safer options. On the contrary, life is about living a life worth living. Therefore, taking risks will be part of being courageous, which is the royal road to wisdom. That is the way you will acquire this unusual kind of knowledge. That is the way you will become a reflective leader.

Naturally, there is always a good probability that when you stand for what you think is right you may not succeed, but at least everyone will know what you stood for. Is not staying silent when you ought to speak up comparable to a slow growing cancer within your soul? If truth be told, there will be times in life when you can choose courage or you can choose comfort, but you cannot choose both, and I would like to add that making the wrong choice may be better than making no choice at all.

Furthermore, you should also realize that courage can be contagious. Every time you are brave, it is quite likely that you are also making the people around you a little braver. Mirroring can be an extremely important influence on other people's behavior when they find themselves in threatening situations.[1] When people see courageous examples, they may

---

[1] Giacomo Rizzolatti and Maddalena Fabbri-Destro (2008). The mirror system and its role in social cognition. *Current Opinion in Neurobiology*. 18 (2): 179–184; Marco Iacoboni (2008). *Mirroring People: The New Science of How We Connect with Others*. New York: Picador.

mirror it and follow. Whether you are going to be as brave as the Zen master, described in the following anecdote, however, is another question.

During the civil wars in feudal Japan, an invading army would quickly sweep into a town and take control. In one particular village, everyone fled just before the army arrived – everyone except the wise Zen master. Curious about this old fellow, the general went to the temple to see for himself what kind of person this Zen master was. When he met him, he was not treated with the deference and submissiveness to which he was accustomed, and so the general burst into anger. 'You fool,' he shouted as he reached for his sword, 'don't you realize you are standing before a man who could run you through without blinking an eye!' Despite the threat, the Zen master seemed unmoved. 'And do you realize,' the Zen master replied calmly, 'that you are standing before a man who can be run through without blinking an eye?'

Wise people also realize that if you are not willing to take risks, you will not learn. Thus, to show courage can also be looked at as a developmental journey. To conquer fear will always be a great learning experience. What I am trying to say is that courage and wisdom tend to be closely linked. As the writer Publius Syrus said, 'No one knows what he can do till he tries.' Perhaps there is also some truth in the statement of Friedrich Nietzsche, 'That which doesn't kill us makes us stronger.' Many of the important things in the world have been accomplished by people who had the courage to keep on trying when there seemed to be little or no hope at all. However, if you decide to engage in a courageous activity, remember that courage is like a muscle that will strengthen with its use. Let us now turn to the story of three pots.

Once upon a time, a daughter complained to her father that her life was miserable and that she did not know how she was going to manage in the future.

She said that she was tired of fighting and struggling all the time. It looked like when one problem was solved, another one soon followed.

Her father, a well-known chef, took her to the kitchen. He filled three pots with water and placed each on a high fire.

Once the three pots began to boil, he placed potatoes in one pot, eggs in the second pot and ground coffee beans in the third pot. He then let them sit and boil, without saying a word to his daughter.

The daughter impatiently waited, wondering what her father was trying to do. After twenty minutes he turned off the burners.

He took the potatoes out of the pot and placed them in a bowl. He pulled the eggs out and placed them in another bowl. He then ladled the coffee out and placed it in a cup.

Turning to her, he asked. 'Daughter, what do you see?'

'Potatoes, eggs and coffee,' she hastily replied.

'Come closer' he said, 'and touch the potatoes.' She did and noted that they were soft.

He then asked her to take an egg and break it. After pulling off the shell, she told her father that it was hard-boiled.

Finally, he asked her to sip the coffee. Its rich aroma brought a smile to her face.

'Father, what are you trying to tell me?' she asked him.

He then explained that the potatoes, the eggs and coffee beans had each faced the same adversity: the boiling water. However, each one reacted differently. The potato went in strong, hard and unrelenting, but in boiling water, it became soft and weak.

The egg was fragile, with the thin outer shell protecting its liquid interior until it was put in the boiling water. Then the inside of the egg became hard.

However, the ground coffee beans were unique. After they were exposed to the boiling water, they changed the water and created something new.

'Which one do you want to be?' he asked his daughter. 'When adversity knocks on your door, how do you respond? Are you going to be a potato, an egg or a coffee bean? Will you act courageously? Will the experience be transformative?'

What next?

Courage requires action. With that in mind, next time when you are facing a difficult situation, why don't you challenge yourself? Why don't you act out your dreams? Remember, without dreams, there is no courage, and without courage, there is no action. So, why not be brave? Why not let go of your need for comfort and security? Why not accept a degree of uncertainty? In fact, certainty can be like a prison. So, why don't you break free and you'll be free. To quote Seneca, 'It's not because things are difficult that we do not dare, it is because we do not dare that things are difficult.' As you may have realized, you are not born with courage, but you are born with the potential for courage. However, not being courageous means staying in your comfort zone – preferring the familiarity, safety and routine of your daily life. Courage, on the other hand, is the power to let go of the familiar – to put your vulnerability on the line. The story of the young eagle may shed further light on what I am trying to say.

There once was a hunter who found an abandoned eagle egg. Concerned for the life within, he brought the egg home to his farm and placed it with a few chicken eggs. In due time, the baby eagle hatched from its shell alongside a few of the chicks. The baby eagle began its life just like the chicks, sheltered by the mother hen. As the baby eagle matured, it ate, strutted and even tried to 'cluck' and 'cackle' like a chicken.

One day as a bald eagle flew over the hunter's farm, he saw the little eagle mingling together with the other chickens. He flew down to talk to the young eagle. As the bald eagle landed, all the terrified chickens ran away. As the young eagle tried to run away, he was stopped by the bald eagle. The bald eagle asked, 'What are you doing here among all these chickens? You are an eagle! You can fly and your home is high up among the cliffs!' The young eagle did not know how to respond. He could not accept the fact that he was an eagle. He answered, 'I can't fly, I am a chicken! This is where I belong, close to the ground!'

The bald eagle became impatient. He grabbed the young eagle in his claws and flew to a nearby cliff. As they rested on the cliff, the bald eagle said, 'You are an eagle. I know you can fly!' and with a mighty swish of his wings, the bald eagle carried the young eagle up into the clouds. Once they soared high above the clouds, the bald eagle dropped the young eagle as he yelled, 'Flap your wings and fly! You're an eagle!' Then the young eagle, to his bewilderment, flapped his wings and discovered that he could fly.

If we try, we can awaken the eagle inside. All of us have the potential to soar high above the clouds. However, many of us may be too 'chicken', not daring to leave the ground, not realizing the great potential that resides within us.

As a way of moving forward, of being courageous, write down five things you would do in your life if you had absolutely no fear. Then pick one of them and do it. As part of this exercise, you could also ask yourself, who is the most courageous individual you have personally known. Also, is there some courageous person in history whom you identify with? What were the reasons that you have chosen these individuals?

While keeping in mind what you have learned from this exercise, what is really stopping you from moving forward? Why not try to do what you may be capable of? Why not try to be courageous – and take risks? Thus, why not stop being a chicken today!

11

Happiness

Our happiness depends on wisdom all the way.

—Sophocles

Rules for happiness: something to do, someone to love, something to hope for.

—Immanuel Kant

Lesson 8: Happiness

Nasrudin saw a traveller sitting disconsolately at the wayside. He asked, what is the matter?

'There is nothing of interest in life,' said the traveller. 'I have a lot of money. I don't need to work. I am on this trip only in order to seek something more interesting than the life I have at home. So far, I haven't been lucky. I haven't found happiness.'

Without another word, Nasrudin seized the traveller's backpack and made off down the road with it, running like a gazelle. Since he knew the area, he was able to easily outdistance him. The road curved, and Nasrudin cut across several loops, with the result that he was soon back on the road ahead of the man whom he had robbed. He put the bag by the side of the road and waited behind some bushes for the other to catch up.

Presently the miserable traveller appeared, following the tortuous road, more unhappy than ever because of the loss of his backpack. As soon as he saw his property lying there, he ran towards it. After opening the bag, seeing that everything was still there, he shouted with joy.

'Isn't that a rather simple way of producing happiness?' observed Nasrudin.

The Roman emperor Marcus Aurelius said, 'The happiness of your life depends upon the quality of your thoughts.' According to him, it is not what you have, or who you are, or where you are, or what you are doing that makes you happy or unhappy. It is how you think. The theologian Albert Schweitzer was wittier when saying, 'Happiness is nothing more than good health and a bad memory.'

Wise people have realized, however, that much happiness is not out there; it is to be found within you. Perhaps you are just as happy as you make up your mind to be. You may not really be aware of it, but you should know that you have some control over your own happiness. Although you cannot control the world, you can try to control your own reactions to whatever is happening to you. It is always good to remind yourself that your attitude towards what is happening to you is going to be your choice.

What I am trying to say is that you should not rely on others for your happiness. You should not give other people the power to control your mind, your life and your happiness. After all, if you do not take control of your own life, someone else is bound to do so. Your happiness is going to be your responsibility. Thus, to be happy is very much a question of attitude – a reflection of your state of mind. You can nearly always enjoy things if you make up your mind that you want to do so. It is not what you have or who you are or where you are or what you are doing that decides whether you are happy or unhappy. Most often, it is how you think about these matters, but *you* have to take responsibility.

Until you make peace with who you are, however, you will never be content with what you have. As I am suggesting, there is only one cause of unhappiness: it is how you think about yourself. It implies that you have to recognize your qualities. You have to learn to appreciate yourself. Do not turn into a divided self. You have to learn to accept who you are – with all the good and the bad. It is something you should not leave up to others. If you do not like what you see looking at yourself, you need to make the changes in your life as *you* see fit – not because you believe someone else wants you to be different. The ancient Chinese philosopher Lao Tzu said it quite pointedly: 'If you look to others for fulfillment, you will never be fulfilled. If your happiness depends on money, you will never be happy with yourself. Be content with what you have; rejoice in the way things are. When you realize there is nothing lacking, the world belongs to you.' You should not forget that happiness does not come as a result of being obsessed about things you do not have, but rather by recognizing and appreciating what you do have. A significant part of your happiness is all up to you.

The hedonic treadmill

Concerning your happiness, the question becomes: what is the hedonic treadmill doing to you? How are you dealing with the positive and negative changes that are occurring in your life? Are there ways in which you can influence this hedonic treadmill?

The hedonic treadmill is a metaphor for the idea that your degree of happiness tends to return to where it was originally, regardless of good fortune or the negative life events that we have experienced.[1] Apparently, you have a happiness set point, which refers to your subjectively determined predisposition for happiness. In other words, whatever the happiness trigger may be, you have a tendency to return to your original happiness set point after a short period of time. This is also true for happy events, as well as dreadful things that may have happened to you. Human beings have a remarkable ability to recover from even the most terrible losses or traumas.[2]

However, although genetics and personality variables may largely explain your hedonic set point, your goals and attentional focus also play a role in your day-to-day happiness experience. Generally speaking – probably due to the influence of evolutionary forces – your affect balance scores (positive and negative moods and emotions) tend to be above

[1] Philip Brickman and Donald Campbell (1971). Hedonic relativism and planning the good society. In M. H. Appley (ed.), *Adaptation-Level Theory*. New York: Academic Press. pp. 287–305.

[2] Shane Frederick and George Loewenstein (1999). Hedonic adaptation. In Daniel Kahneman, Edward Diener, and Norbert Schwarz (eds). *Well-Being: Foundations of Hedonic Psychology*. New York, NY: Russell Sage Foundation. pp. 302–329.

neutral. If they were below neutral, they would endanger your wish to continue living.

In fact, research by the positive psychologist Sonja Lyubomirsky indicates that 50 per cent of your happiness is genetic, 10 per cent is based on life circumstances and 40 per cent is under your control.[3] Therefore, what these figures point out is that you can do something about your happiness, but only if you are prepared to make the effort to do so. In other words, if you want to, you do not have to be stuck on the treadmill – you can change your score on the happiness equation.[4] To focus on the positive and to be grateful for what you have can make quite a difference. In fact, having a positive attitude towards life can function as a real happiness magnet. Thus, if you live life with a positive attitude, it is more likely that good things and good people will be drawn to you. You may even discover that happiness can be contagious.

In other words, a happy person is not merely a person subjected to a certain set of circumstances, but also a person with a certain set of attitudes. Therefore, happiness, like unhappiness, seems to be somewhat of a proactive choice. To be more specific, you should try to grow your happiness in your own garden. You would also do well to remind yourself that an extremely important part of the happiness equation is that you tend to live longer if you have a more optimistic, happy outlook to life. Experiencing happiness seems to be associated with a longer life expectancy. In fact, one elaborate

---

[3] Sonja Lyubomirsky (2007). *The How of Happiness: A New Approach to Getting the Life You Want*. New York: Penguin Books.

[4] Manfred F. R. Kets de Vries (2007). *The Happiness Equation*. London: Ebury Publishing.

study concerning happiness found a 14.9 per cent longer life span for women in the highest optimism quartile. For men, the figure was 10.9 per cent.[5]

A state of mind

What I am trying to emphasize is that happiness does not come as a result of getting something you do not have, but rather by recognizing and appreciating what you do have. As you may have discovered by now, you cannot buy happiness. There is no correlation between happiness and how much money you have. In fact, money has never made people happy. Money is not the solution to your problems. The best you can say is that it lets you carry your unhappiness around in a more glorious style. Far too often, however, you can see that many people born to wealth – who have the means of gratifying every wish they have – are not happy. When you really think about it, money means numbers and these numbers will never end. Often, it is sadly true that the more money you have, the more you may want. Also, when comparing your wealth with that of others, as you may have discovered, there is always someone who is going to be richer. Thus, if you believe that it takes money to make you happy, your search for happiness will be never ending.

As I suggested before, real happiness is an inner quality; it is a quality of thought, a state of mind. It is not a possession.

[5] Lewina O. Lee, Peter James, Emily S. Zevon, Eric S. Kim, Claudia Trudel-Fitzgerald, Avron Spiro, Francine Grodstein and Laura D. Kubzansky (2019). Optimism is associated with exceptional longevity in 2 epidemiologic cohorts of men and women. *Proceedings of the National Academy of Sciences of the United States of America*, 116 (37), 18357–18362.

In fact, without possessions, but when your mind is at peace, you can be quite happy. However, if you have everything the world can give you, but lack peace of mind, you are never going to be happy. In short, happiness is very much based on appreciating what you have – meaning having good relationships with others, enjoying what you do, having choice, finding purpose and having meaning in life.

What is also helpful to remember is that happiness does not mean that everything is going to be perfect. Actually, perfectionism often will be the enemy of happiness. Therefore, as I have mentioned earlier, it is wiser to look beyond life's imperfections. Blaming others when things go wrong is also not a prescription for happiness. Bad things will happen to all of us. You will feel much better about your life, however, when you decide that you own your problems and that it is up to you to do something about them. In other words, wise people take responsibility for their own happiness. They never hand it over to others. Thus, stop blaming your problems on your mother, your father, your wife, your husband, the people at work, your friends or even the politicians that affect your life. Always remind yourself that you have some control over your own destiny.

Of course, during your life, you will have setbacks, sometimes due to events that are not under your control. Similarly, there are going to be situations where you will turn out to be the author of your own misery. However, instead of complaining, welcome these setbacks and imperfections. Try to learn from them. Do not waste your time on anger, regrets, worries and grudges. And as I described in Chapter 5, learn to forgive. It is important to remind yourself that the only person you hurt when you stay angry or hold on to grudges will be you. The secret of being happy is accepting where you are in life and making the most out of every day. This brings to mind the celebrated quote from Johann Strauss's famous operetta, *Die Fledermaus* (*The Bat*): '*Glücklich ist, wer vergisst, was doch nicht zu ändern ist*', sometimes translated as 'Happy is he who forgets what cannot be changed'. Thus, do not start worrying about the things you cannot change. Instead, try to focus your energy on the things that you can change.

Alignment

Mahatma Gandhi once said, 'Happiness is when what you think, what you say, and what you do are in harmony.' Much of the conflict you have in your life exists simply because you are not living your life in alignment; you are not being true to yourself. You are living too much the life of a divided self. You put on too much of a mask, a persona. If you find yourself in such a situation, however, you need to calibrate, readjust and get rid of your negative energy. Deal with the shadow side inside you. Neutralize it. Fill your life with positive energy. As a path to wisdom, you should know that it is much better to laugh at life than to turn life into a tragedy.

Of course, misanthropes, given their mindset, would say that happiness is a mere distraction from the human tragedy. However, as I have suggested before, the greater part of your happiness or misery depends upon your disposition and not upon your circumstances. Happiness is not having what you want. It is appreciating what you have. You can nearly always enjoy things if you firmly make up your mind that that is what you want to do. Also keep in mind that part of the happiness equation is to enjoy your own life without comparing it with that of someone else. As I explained in Chapters 6 and 7, envy and greed can be great spoilers of your happiness. Seeking to build your own happiness on the unhappiness of others leads to a very shaky foundation.

Happiness and sadness

Some people look at happiness as the interval between periods of unhappiness, and naturally, even a happy life cannot be without a measure of darkness. After all, if you have not experienced pain and unhappiness, how would you otherwise know when you are happy. Constant happiness could be looked at like a kind of madness. It would have a manic quality.

Conversely, some people would rather be certain that they remain miserable, than to take the risk of becoming happy, but, as I have said before, happiness is very much a choice. Ultimately, happiness comes down to choosing between the discomfort of becoming aware of your psychological issues vis-à-vis the discomfort of being ruled by them. To repeat myself, face your inner demons. It is up to you not to love with a divided self. It is up to you to create a greater sense of authenticity and, given the fact that life will bring you pain all by itself, it is also your responsibility to create joy. Thus, try to reflect upon your present blessings, of which every person has many – not on your past misfortunes, of which we all have some. In sum, you do not find the happy life. You have to help create it.

Ironically, sometimes the search for happiness can also become one of the chief sources of unhappiness. It could turn into an obsession. For some people, nothing seems to be good enough in life. To be able to be truly happy always seems to escape them. However, it very well may be that the moment they stop trying so hard to be happy, they could have a pretty good time. Here the story of the Old Man may provide us with some clues.

An Old Man lived in the village. He was one of the most unhappy people anyone could think of. Given his constant moaning about his unhappiness, the whole village had become very tired of him. The Old Man was always gloomy; he was always in a bad mood and sadly enough, the longer he lived, the more misanthropic he was becoming. To deal with him had become more and more toxic. Everyone in the village avoided him as his unhappiness was contagious.

But one day, when he turned eighty, an incredible thing happened. The rumor went around: 'The Old Man is happy today; he doesn't complain about anything; he smiles; he looks very different.'

All the villagers gathered at his house to see him. When he stepped out of the door, the old man was asked, 'What happened to you?'

He responded, 'Nothing special. Eighty years I've been chasing happiness, and it was useless. And then I decided to live without happiness and just enjoy the moment. That's why I'm happy now.'

Happiness as a journey

As the above story illustrates, happiness is not necessarily achieved by the conscious pursuit of happiness; it is generally the by-product, and a pleasant one, of a life lived well. As we have experienced ourselves, happiness can be very ethereal. It comes and goes. The novelist Nathaniel

Hawthorne once said, 'Happiness is like a butterfly which, when pursued, is always beyond our grasp, but, if you will sit down quietly, may alight upon you.' As has become clear by now, happiness is also a manner of travelling. Unfortunately, plenty of people missed their share of happiness, not because they never found it, but because they did not stop in their journey through life to enjoy the moments. Thus, learning how to create and appreciate happy moments makes for a life well lived. In other words, you need to focus on the journey, not on the destination. Often, as you may also have found out, the art of being happy lies in the power of extracting happiness from common things.

Happiness now

As the saying goes, the foolish man seeks happiness in the distance, the wise grows it under his feet. In other words, try to be happy right now. People are always worried about what is happening next. They often find it difficult to stand still, to occupy the now without worrying about the future. Thus, if you want to be happy, do not dwell in the past; do not worry so much about the future, but focus on living fully in the present. The French novelist Marcel Pagnol concurred when he said, 'The reason people find it so hard to be happy is that they always see the past better than it was, the present worse than it is, and the future less resolved than it will be.'

You should recognize that happiness is always to be found in these special moments that come and go. Unfortunately, when these special moments occur, you may not even be aware of them. Only afterwards may you discover that these moments brought you happiness. Thus, you should avoid postponing happiness for the future. On the contrary, it is something you design for the present. Plenty of people miss their share of happiness, not because they never found it, but because they never bothered to enjoy it while travelling. Always pay homage to *carpe diem* – seize the day or, more literally, 'pluck the day [as it is ripe]'. Thus, if you are wise, you plan your life like you will live forever but live your life like you will die the next day.

Oscar Wilde once said facetiously, 'Some cause happiness wherever they go; others whenever they go.' In other words, you would do yourself a tremendous favor to stay away from the people who poison your spirit. In the pursuit of happiness, it is wise to distance yourself from argumentative, negative people who try to pull you down. These toxic people will suck the energy out of you; they impede your progress.

If happiness is important to you, you should give preference to people who look at the world with a dose of optimism, people who can inspire you, people who can make you happy and also people who will provide you with peace of mind. Keep in mind that although you cannot change all the people around you, at least you can change the people you choose to be around. Life is too short to waste your time on people who do not respect, appreciate and value you. It is much better to spend your life with people who make you smile, laugh and feel loved.

The altruistic motive

The famous writer and stateman Johann Wolfgang von Goethe once noted, 'Who is the happiest of men? He who values the merits of others, and in their pleasure takes joy, even as though it were his own.' In the happiness equation, a way to increase your happiness is to bring happiness to others.[6] By and large, altruistic acts raise your mood because they raise your self-esteem, which in turn increases your degree of happiness. Furthermore, altruistic activities get you outside of yourself. These activities will distract you from your own problems. As a matter of fact, your happiness will increase when you do things for people not because of who they are or what they do in return, but because of who you are. After all, it is hard not to feel happy when you make someone else smile. There is no true happiness in having or in getting, but only in giving. In more than one way, happiness is only true happiness when it is shared.

Thus, in your pursuit of happiness, you should always try to find opportunities to make someone else smile, to offer random acts of kindness in everyday life. You should give often but take rarely. Remind yourself that people will forget what you said. People will forget what you did. But people will never forget how you made them feel. If you are not making someone else's life better, then you are wasting your time. Now let us consider the tale of the mouse and mousetrap.

> *A mouse looked through the crack in the wall to see the farmer and his wife open a package. 'Could there be food in that package?' the mouse wondered. He was totally devastated discovering that it was a mousetrap.*

---

[6] Sonja Lyubomirsky (2007). *The How of Happiness: A Scientific Approach to Getting the Life You Want*. New York, NY: The Penguin Press.

Retreating to the farmyard, the mouse proclaimed the warning: 'I'm so scared, there is a mousetrap in the house! There is a mousetrap in the house!'

The chicken clucked and scratched, raised her head and said, 'Mr. Mouse, I can see that this is a grave concern to you, but it is of no consequence to me. Don't bother me with it.'

The mouse turned to the pig and told him, 'There is a mousetrap in the house! There is a mousetrap in the house!' The pig sympathized, but said, 'I am so very sorry, Mr. Mouse, but there is nothing I can do about it but pray. I will mention you in my prayers.'

The mouse turned to the cow and said, 'There is a mousetrap in the house! There is a mousetrap in the house!' The cow said, 'That's terrible, Mr. Mouse. I'm sorry for you, but it's not my problem.'

So, the mouse returned to the house, head down and dejected, to face the farmer's mousetrap alone. There was nobody willing to offer help.

That very night a sound was heard throughout the house – like the sound of a mousetrap catching its prey. The farmer's wife rushed to see what was caught. In the darkness, she did not see that it was a highly venomous snake whose tail had got caught in the trap. The snake then bit the farmer's wife. The farmer rushed her to the hospital and she returned home with a fever.

Everyone knows that the best way to treat a fever is with chicken soup, so the farmer took his hatchet to the farmyard for the soup's main ingredient, but his wife's sickness continued, so friends and neighbors came to sit with her around the clock. To feed all these people, the farmer decided to butcher the pig. The farmer's wife's health deteriorated even more and she died. So many people came to her funeral that the farmer needed to provide for all the visitors, making him decide to slaughter the cow.

> *While all these things were going on, the mouse looked upon all these developments from his hole in the wall with great sadness. If only all the other animals had paid notice. If only they had been kinder.*

As I tried to explain in Chapter 4, random acts of kindness, no matter how small, can make a tremendous impact on someone else's life. It can make them happy and their happiness may rub off. So, the next time you hear someone is facing a problem and you think it does not concern you, remember: when one of us is threatened, we are all at risk. We are all involved in this journey called life. We must keep an eye out for one another and make an extra effort to encourage one another. Each of us is a vital thread in another person's tapestry.

In particular, what adds to the happiness equation is to spend energy on a worthy purpose. The happiest people are those who lose themselves in the service of others. Often, the secret of happiness is to find something more important than you are and dedicate your life to it. When you are living the best version of yourself, you inspire others to also live the best versions of themselves.

Expressing gratitude

In addition to feeling happy, there is always the power of gratitude – the readiness to show appreciation for and to return kindness. It is a funny thing about life that once you begin to take note of the things you are grateful for, you begin to lose sight of the things that you lack. Gratitude unlocks the fullness of life. It can be looked at as another key to happiness. It turns what you have into enough, and more. Gratitude makes sense of your past, brings peace for today and creates a vision for tomorrow.

Sometimes, I wonder whether to attain real happiness, you have to be somewhat of a Buddhist. It is noted that the Buddha said: 'Learn to let go. That is the key to happiness.' The message is that wise people are modest about their needs. As I suggested in Chapter 7, greed is not one of their qualities. Envy is not either. In other words, you should just let things pass through your life without getting entangled with them. Thus, according to the Buddha, to end the suffering that is life, you need to give up all attachments and expectations. To be able to accept things as they are is a way to let go of your unmet desires. Thus, letting go will give you freedom and freedom is the only condition for happiness. However, if you cling to anything, you can never be free. At the same time, letting go does not mean that you do not care about anyone and anything. You love life fully but without clinging to it for your survival. Therefore, the paradox of happiness implies that until you can accept what is, you cannot move into what might be. Therefore, create happy moments for yourself, starting today. It will make you more effective in whatever you do.

12

Conclusion

Am I a man of great wisdom? Hardly! Even when a simple person brings me a question, my mind goes utterly blank. I just thrash it out until I've exhausted every possibility.

—Confucius

He who lives in harmony with himself lives in harmony with the universe.

—Marcus Aurelius

Letting go

When Alexander the Great appeared before the Greek leaders in Corinth, they greeted him warmly and paid him lavish compliments – all of them, but one, a philosopher called Diogenes. He had views not unlike those of the Buddha. According to him, possessions and all the things we think we need only serve to distract us. They get in the way of life's enjoyment. By sticking to his extremely simple lifestyle, Diogenes was criticizing the social values and institutions of what he saw as a corrupt, confused society. To provide a living example of his principles, he had given away everything he owned. He turned poverty into a virtue. He begged for a living. He would spend his time almost naked, living on the market square and sleeping in a large ceramic barrel.

Very curious to meet this strange fellow, Alexander went out to call on him. Dressed in his shining armor, the plume on his helmet waving in the wind, he walked up to the barrel and said to Diogenes: 'Is there any favor I can do for you. Let me know your wish and I shall grant it.'

Diogenes, who had until then been comfortably warming himself in the sun, replied: 'Indeed, Sire, I do have a wish.'

'Well, what is it?' Alexander replied.

'Your shadow has fallen over me. Can you stand a little less between me and the sun?'

Alexander is said to have been so struck by this response that he said: 'If I weren't Alexander, I should like to be Diogenes.'

'If I were not Diogenes, I would still wish to be Diogenes,' Diogenes supposedly replied.

As Diogenes would say, 'It is the privilege of the gods to want nothing and of god-like men to want little. When what we are is what we want to be, that could also be a way to describe wisdom. Furthermore, letting go of all attachments may be another way of attaining wisdom. As mentioned in the previous chapter, the Buddha abandoned everything that he knew and loved in order to seek wisdom and enlightenment, a state of being that has defined the Buddhist traditions. Throughout his life, the search for wisdom would be guiding his actions. Wisdom made him take wise choices in life and his practiced wisdom turned out to be beneficial for the common good. No wonder that the Buddha's ideas about wisdom have stood the test of time.

Of course, the Buddhas of this world will be very hard to find, but that does not mean that during the journey that is your life, you cannot develop a degree of wisdom to make your life more fulfilling, and also better for the people around you. I do realize in saying this that choosing this path will not be easy. It will always be a challenge to be wise in words and also in deeds. However, the legacy you leave is the life you lead.

Wisdom implies that you have found harmony between your inner and outer world. As I mentioned repeatedly, to always have to put on a persona or a mask – to have to live with a divided self – is not the answer, but to be able to integrate these different parts of the self can be difficult. Dealing with your shadow side is always going to be a challenge and repressing these aspects of yourself will also not be the answer. Integrating these aspects of yourself will make you feel better in your skin. In addition, from a developmental perspective, to be open to new experiences will help you grow, and if you can maintain your curiosity about the happenings around you, you will be able to learn from experience. It could mean, however, that you have to get out of your comfort zone. After all, if you do what you have always done, you will get what you have always achieved.

Wise people recognize that life moves with an ebb and a flow. There will be highs and lows and there will be peaks and valleys. Life is never going to be an easy ride, but during this journey that is your life there can be discovery, change and growth if that is what you seek. During this journey, you can have a choice: you can acquire wisdom or you can remain blinded. What you decide to do is all up to you.

This journey towards wisdom very much implies living in the present, planning for the future, and profiting from the past. It is all about finding the most suitable ways to integrate your life's experiences. During this journey, you may also discover what you need to unlearn. Doing so will be a challenge, but hopefully, while you are journeying, the art of growing old graciously will be part of your wisdom equation.

Unfortunately, as I mentioned previously, growing old wisely is not a given. As Benjamin Franklin noted: 'Life's tragedy is that we get old too soon and wise too late.' However, could it not very well be that you need to be first young and stupid to become old and wise? Whatever the situation, you should learn how to live wisely the time that has been given to you.

At the same time, while seeking the wisdom of the ages, you should also try to retain your ability to interpret the world through the eyes of a child. Their sense of wonder will always be unsurpassable. After all, it is children who often ask the questions that intelligent people do not know how to answer. As we know, the curiosity about not knowing is the entry door towards wisdom, but that wisdom is like a very delicate flower. It can very easily wilt. In our pursuit of wisdom, there will be many hiccups. As I have suggested before, we can easily regress, thereby resorting to more base motives. No wonder that the 'desert fathers', these early Christian hermits, introduced the notion of the seven deadly sins, also known as the capital vices – pride, greed, wrath, envy, lust, gluttony, and sloth. Obviously, they were concerned about how easily human beings would slide down the slippery slope of excess. Long before them, the ancient Greek philosophers were also preoccupied with these forces of regression – what could go wrong in the pursuit of wisdom. They wondered how easily human beings would go astray and how easily they would resort to very basic behavior patterns, the seven cardinal sins being prime representations. Clearly, they had much concern about the darker side of human nature.

The ring of power

One of the great passages in Plato's *Republic* concerns the debate concerning 'The Ring of Gyges', a ring that inspired many, among them J.R.R. Tolkien in his fantasy works *The Hobbit* and *The Lord of the Rings*. In this philosophical treatise, Glaucon (the brother of Plato) presents a myth (jointly examined by him and Socrates) and used it as the basis for a discussion on the darker sides of human nature. Glaucon was trying to make the point that, by their very nature, human beings tend to be selfish and unjust.

The myth tells us how once in the ancient kingdom of Lydia, there lived a man called Gyges, a shepherd who was in the service of the king of the land. One day, quite by chance, he found a ring that could make him invisible when he turned it one way on his finger and visible again when he turned it the other direction. We learn how Gyges used the ring's magical properties cunningly to conduct a series of crimes that would eventually make him the king of the land. Thus, making himself invisible, he managed to creep into the queen's bedroom, and succeeded in seducing her. With her help, he was able to kill the king. Subsequently, Gyges married the queen and became king himself and, supposedly, they lived happily ever after.

Naturally, Gyges' 'stellar' career raises a number of ethical questions. As the ring made him invisible, he was protected from the consequences of his actions. Nobody knew it was him who had committed these terrible crimes. Thereupon, during the philosophical discussion described in Plato's *The Republic*, the question was put forth as to how wise people would act if they were in possession of such a ring. If they did not have to fear any negative consequences for committing injustices, would they still act wisely or would they regress? Would more base motivations get the upper hand?

According to Glaucon, most people, when invisible, would act unjustly, it being considered as the most rational choice. According to him, only a fool would act in a morally responsible way when unobserved. In fact, to act in a morally responsible way should be seen as an irrational act, as people supposedly only do the right thing if they cannot get away with their wrongdoings.

This disturbing thought experiment points to the darker side of *Homo sapiens*. It shows how easily human beings go down a dark, slippery slope. In essence, this dialogue in *The Republic* tries to answer the question: Does self-interest override morality? Will wisdom yield to self-interest? Clearly, what this myth is trying to demonstrate is that the possession of this ring unleashes the real truth about human nature. It points out that most people are inherently self-interested. Doing something for the common good is merely an afterthought. What is more, to have people act in a wise manner is nothing more than an illusion. Human beings, if given the chance, are always going to satisfy their basic passions, will follow their instincts and will act in this way without concern for the well-being of others. Sadly enough, if Glaucon was right, people would do whatever they think they could get away with. They would not act wisely, not taking into consideration the greater good.

Concerned about this conclusion, the statesman and writer Cicero retold the story of Gyges in his treatise *De Officiis*. According to him, wise or good individuals would base their decisions on a 'fear of moral degradation' as opposed to punishment or negative consequences. Basically, he argues that, if you possess a strong moral compass, the ring of Gyges is not necessarily going to lead you astray. The pursuit of wisdom is not merely an exercise in the absurd.

Perhaps, even though I may sound naive, I tend to agree with Cicero. Although I am very cognizant of the darker side of human nature, throughout this book I have argued that if there is congruence between how you show yourself to the outside world and how you experience your inner world – if you are not experiencing a significantly divided self – Gyges' ring will not have much of an effect on you. It is more likely that you will continue to live according to your value system. In that respect, it may very well be true that character is destiny. If you know yourself, if you have a good sense of what you stand for, if you have a strong sense of values, you are more likely to stay the course. You will be more likely to transcend the self, taking the common good into consideration.

Thus, idealistic as I may sound, for people who have their house in order – who have acquired a degree of wisdom – to possess the ring of Gyges should not lead them astray. Knowing what they are all about – having a sense of integrity and authenticity – will make the possessing of the ring inconsequential with respect to how they live their lives. They have always been living their lives with a modicum of harmony and there has always been congruence between the inner and outer self.

Furthermore, if, like Socrates, you have attained a degree of wisdom, you may not even have a desire to possess such a ring. Of course, if your inner life is very different from your outer life – if you live a divided life – possessing this ring of power could bring out the worst in you. You may very well be tempted to behave like Gyges.

This myth begs the question: after having read this treatise on wisdom, would you wish to continue living life with a divided self, acting like Gyges or would you want to be different? In other words, what would *you* do if you found this ring? Would you do what is right or what is easy? Would you find ways to handle this ring in a 'wise' manner?

As I have said repeatedly in this book, the gateway to wisdom is knowing yourself. Self-knowledge has always been the royal road to wisdom. During these inner travels, no one, from the very mighty to the very humble, has a monopoly on what road to take.

However, if you are able to make the best of this inner journey, you can show wisdom in the way that you live your life. It will be shown through the appropriate use of knowledge. It will be shown through the judgements you make. It will be reflected in your capacity for empathy and compassion and it will be shown through your action as a leader at whatever level. Although this nobler journey may be difficult, it is nonetheless worth your effort. To stay stagnant is not the answer. You may want to heed the warning of Confucius, 'Only the wisest and stupidest of men never change.' There comes a moment in history when ignorance is no longer acceptable. There comes a moment when only wisdom has the power to absolve and it is through wisdom that we can create a better world.

About the Author

Manfred F. R. Kets de Vries brings a different view to the much-studied subjects of leadership and the psychological dimensions of individual and organizational change. Bringing to bear his knowledge and experience of economics (Econ. Drs, University of Amsterdam), management (ITP, MBA and DBA, Harvard Business School), and psychoanalysis (Membership Canadian Psychoanalytic Society, Paris Psychoanalytic Society and the International Psychoanalytic Association), he explores the interface between management science, psychoanalysis, developmental psychology, evolutionary psychology, neuroscience, psychotherapy, executive coaching and consulting. His specific areas of interest are leadership (the 'bright' and 'dark' side), entrepreneurship, career dynamics, talent management, family business, cross-cultural management, succession planning, organizational and individual stress, C-suite team building, executive coaching, organizational development, transformation management and management consulting.

The Distinguished Clinical Professor of Leadership Development and Organizational Change at INSEAD, he is Program Director of INSEAD's top management program, 'The Challenge of Leadership: Creating Reflective Leaders', and the Founder of INSEAD's Executive Master Program in Change Management. He has also been the founder of INSEAD's Global Leadership Center.

Furthermore, he has been a pioneer in team coaching. As an educator, he has received INSEAD's distinguished MBA teacher award six times. He has held professorships at McGill University, the École des Hautes Études Commerciales, Montreal, the European School for Management and Technology (ESMT), Berlin, and the Harvard Business School. He has lectured at management institutions around the world. *The Financial Times*, *Le Capital*, *Wirtschaftswoche* and *The Economist* have rated Manfred Kets de Vries among the world's leading management thinkers and among the most influential contributors to human resource management.

Kets de Vries is the author, co-author or editor of more than 50 books, including *The Neurotic Organization*, *Organizational Paradoxes*, *Struggling with the Demon: Perspectives on Individual and Organizational Irrationality*, *Fools, Leaders and Impostors*, *Life and Death in the Executive Fast Lane*, *Prisoners of Leadership*, *The Leadership Mystique*, *The Happiness Equation*, *Are Leaders Made or Are They Born?: The Case of Alexander the Great*, *The New Russian Business Elite*, *Leadership by Terror: Finding Shaka Zulu in the Attic*, *The Leader on the Couch*, *Coach and Couch*, *The Family Business on the Couch*, *Sex, Money, Happiness, and Death: The Quest for Authenticity*, *Reflections on Leadership and Character*, *Reflections on Leadership and Career*, *Reflections on Organizations*, *The Coaching Kaleidoscope*, *The Hedgehog Effect: The Secrets of High Performance Teams*, *Mindful Leadership Coaching: Journeys into the Interior*, *You Will Meet a Tall Dark Stranger: Executive Coaching Challenges*, *Telling Fairy Tales in the Boardroom: How to Make Sure Your Organization Lives Happily Ever After*, *Riding the Leadership Roller Coaster: A Psychological Observer's Guide*, *Down the Rabbit Hole of Leadership: Leadership Pathology of Everyday Life*, *The CEO Whisperer: Meditations on Leaders, Life and Change*, *Quo Vadis: The Existential Challenges of Leaders*, *Leadership Unhinged: Essays on the Ugly, the Bad, and the Weird* and *The Daily Perils of Executive Life: How to Survive when Dancing on Quicksand*.

In addition, Kets de Vries has published more than 400 academic papers as chapters in books and as articles. He has also written approximately 100 case studies, including seven that received the Best Case of the Year award. In addition, he has written hundreds of mini-articles for the *Harvard Business Review*, INSEAD Knowledge and other digital outlets. Furthermore, he has designed various 360-degree feedback instruments including the widely used *Global Executive Leadership Mirror* and the *Organizational Culture Audit*.

Kets de Vries is a regular writer for various magazines. His work has been featured in such publications as *The New York Times*, *The Wall Street Journal*, *The Los Angeles Times*, *Fortune*, *Business Week*, *The Economist*, *The Financial Times* and *The Harvard Business Review*. His books and articles have been translated into more than thirty languages.

Furthermore, Kets de Vries is a member of seventeen editorial boards and is a Fellow of the Academy of Management. He is also a founding member of the International Society for the Psychoanalytic Study of Organizations (ISPSO), which has honored him as a lifetime member.

In addition, Kets de Vries is the first non-US recipient of the International Leadership Association Lifetime Achievement Award for his contributions to leadership research and development (being considered one of the world's founding professionals in the development of leadership as a field and discipline). He received a Lifetime

Achievement Award from Germany for his advancement of executive education. The American Psychological Association has honored him with the 'Harry and Miriam Levinson Award' for his contributions to Organizational Consultation. Furthermore, he is the recipient of the 'Freud Memorial Award' for his work to further the interface between management and psychoanalysis. In addition, he has also received the 'Vision of Excellence Award' from the Harvard Institute of Coaching. Kets de Vries is the first beneficiary of INSEAD's Dominique Héau Award for 'Inspiring Educational Excellence'. He is also the recipient of two honorary doctorates. The Dutch government has made him an Officer in the Order of Oranje Nassau.

Kets de Vries works as a consultant on organizational design/transformation and strategic human resource management for companies worldwide. As an educator and consultant, he has worked in more than forty countries. In his role as a consultant, he is also the founder-chairman of the Kets de Vries Institute (KDVI), a boutique global strategic leadership development consulting firm with associates worldwide (www.kdvi.com).

Kets de Vries was the first fly fisherman in Outer Mongolia (at the time, becoming the world record holder of the Siberian hucho taimen). He is a member of New York's Explorers Club. In his spare time, he can be found in the rainforests or savannas of Central and Southern Africa, the Siberian taiga, the Ussuri Krai, Kamchatka, the Pamir and Altai Mountains, Arnhem Land or within the Arctic Circle.

E-mail: manfred.ketsdevries@insead.edu

Websites: www.ketsdevries.com and www.kdvi.com

Index